Put-Offs and Come-Ons

Put-Offs and Come-Ons

PSYCHOLOGICAL MANEUVERS AND STRATAGEMS

by A. H. Chapman, M.D.

VISITING LECTURER, THE GREATER KANSAS CITY
MENTAL HEALTH FOUNDATION

G. P. PUTNAM'S SONS, NEW YORK

To the memory of a friend
who shunned all maneuvers and stratagems,
Dean Charles Hyde Warren
Late Master of Trumbull College, Yale University

And for Dick and Pamela Chapman,
who encouraged me to write this book

Preface

This book arises out of my years of peering into people in my work as a psychiatrist. Almost everything in this book comes from experience with patients; it deals with their dilemmas, desires, agonies and pleasures, and the ways in which they satisfy their needs. Theory and speculation occupy little space in this book, although, of course, my points of view show through continually.

In a sense, the patients write the book. I am merely their recorder and their student. Many patients stride boldly onto these pages and they tell their stories in detail. Others merge into general discussions of various types of human predicaments and the ways in which people resolve them. We are especially interested in the ways in which people conflict with one another, manipulate one another, vie with one another, make love to one another and annihilate one another.

Just as this book is written *about* people, it is written *for* people. It is written in the hope that from its pages the unwary may learn a little circumspection, the perplexed may get a little clarity, and the miserable may gain a little relief, for the people who read this book are blood brothers to the people who are recorded in it. If, in its light and simple way, this book accomplishes a few of these objectives, it will justify the effort expended in writing it and the time required to read it.

A.H.C.

7

Contents

Put-Offs and Come-Ons

Put-Offs and Come-Ons, and
Maneuvers and Stratagems

The emotional forces which exist among people may be divided into two broad categories: those forces which push people apart, and those forces which draw them together. For example, anger and sexual frigidity are emotional forces which push people apart, and affection and mutual dependence are emotional forces which draw people together. The strengths and interplays of these two broad groups of emotional forces determine the nature of the interpersonal relationships which occur in marriages, family groups, social groups, business organizations and all the other units of which society is composed.

In common words, the forces which drive people apart from each other may be called the *put-off* forces; anger, fear and competitive hostility *put* people *off* from each other. These put-off forces may break up marriages, dig gulfs between parents and children, destroy love affairs and disrupt social and business organizations. Also in common words, the forces which draw people together may be called the *come-on* forces; they bind people to each other and enable them to live and work in reasonable harmony.

The put-off forces usually are more obvious in human relationships than the come-on forces. Anger, rejection, greed, distrust and rasping competition can be identified with greater ease than love and emotional acceptance. The flash of violence is more easily observed than the tender glance. The emotional forces which hold people together, the come-on forces, are varied. Most of them are healthy, but some of them are unhealthy; insecurity, fear and guilt may hold people together as well as love, friendship and common interests. Anxiety, in various circumstances, may either hold people together or drive them apart.

A large part of the study of human relationships breaks down into an analysis of put-off forces and come-on forces and the endless ways in which they combine in different relationships. No interpersonal relationship, whether in the two-person unit of a marriage or the thousand-person relationship of a factory, is purely put-off or come-on. Both types of emotional forces exist in every relationship, and their relative importance is in a state of continual change. Psychiatry, the medical discipline which deals with unhealthy interpersonal relationships, studies these forces in the individual. The sociologist studies them in large groups. The businessman shrewdly manipulates them to produce or merchandise a product, although he may not be articulately aware of what he is doing. The politician uses them to get votes, and he usually is more or less aware of what he is doing. Children use them to manipulate their parents, and parents use them to cope with their children. Human life is a kaleidoscope of changing patterns of put-off and come-on forces. Most people do not understand how they are using them; therein arise possibilities for danger, grief and misery.

This book attempts many things. One of its goals is to help the unwary to see a little more of these forces and to become more aware of how they operate in the life of the person himself and in the lives of the people around him. Awareness helps. It is not a magic light and there are limits to what it can illumine, but it is better than groping in obscurity.

The material of a book usually arises from the total life experiences of the author. However, this book draws heavily on a particular segment of my life, my years of practice in clinical psychiatry.

A psychiatrist peers with peculiar intensity into the lives of people, and he looks with the aid of special insights and training. He scrutinizes the endless variations of interpersonal relationships, and he examines how they formed the child out of the infant and the adult out of the child. He peeks into dark corners where other persons rarely look. Hence, of all the people who study the put-off and come-on forces of life, he spends more time studying them more intensively with more people than any other kind of person. The lives of some of my patients, with their dilemmas, agonies and gratifications, appear in detail in these pages. In other instances composite information from many patients appears in general descriptions of human predicaments and their consequences.

In discussing how the put-off and come-on forces operate in interpersonal relationships, we shall employ the concepts of *maneuvers* and *stratagems*. Maneuvers and stratagems are well-organized patterns of behavior which people use in putting their feelings into action, in getting what they want, in manipulating each other and in satisfying their needs. We shall consider maneuvers and stratagems in detail, for they occupy the largest part of our attention in this book.

A maneuver is a brief, limited interpersonal operation. The individual may use it in his relationship with one person or with a large group of people. It may last from a few minutes to half a day; it rarely lasts longer. As a rule, the person who uses it employs it frequently. It is part of his customary armamentarium for dealing with interpersonal problems. Depending on what kind of maneuver it is, he may use it in one special kind of interpersonal situation or in many kinds of interpersonal situations. The steps in the maneuver are essentially the same each time the individual uses it, and its result is fairly predictable. Thus maneuvers can be classified and named, and a single type of maneuver will occur in many different people.

17

The person employs a maneuver unconsciously; by "unconsciously" we mean that he is not aware of the true emotional forces which motivate him in the act. He camouflages his motivations from himself and from others by a set of superficial rationalizations which seem convincing to the casual observer. In his maneuver the person achieves an emotional release or satisfies a need of some sort. By our definition of a maneuver, this emotional need is unhealthy, for if it were healthy, from an interpersonal point of view, he would not need a maneuver.

Hence, to recapitulate, we define a maneuver as an interpersonal act of relatively short duration by which the person accomplishes an interpersonally unhealthy objective. He is largely or entirely unaware of the emotional forces which motivate him; he covers his true motivations with rationalizations which are consciously more acceptable to him than his true motivations would be. The steps in the maneuver are the same each time it is used, and its result is predictable. The nature of a maneuver becomes clearer by giving a specific example in detail; we shall present the maneuver of Whine and Decline.

Whine and Decline: A Maneuver

This maneuver is occasionally encountered in sexually frigid women. When a woman who finds sexual intercourse distasteful senses that her husband is going to make sexual advances to her, she begins a discussion on a topic that is a well-known sore point between the two of them. The topic may involve their finances, differences over the children, complaints about the husband's mother, and so forth. She may begin with such opening remarks as, "I know you don't like to discuss it, but I think we really must decide something about . . ." and she sails into the explosive issue flying the colors of well-meaning, innocent devotion to family harmony and the resolution of its problems. From long experience she unconsciously knows just how to goad her husband into a rising storm of irritability with further remarks such as, "The only way to settle this problem is to talk it out like two reasonable people," or "The longer we wait, the worse it will get," or "I have waited until now to talk about this, because you are in a good mood now and seem affectionate toward me."

As she probes further into the sore subject, her husband begins to say some angry things. Thereupon the wife begins to Whine, "I was only trying to help," or "Why do you always get mad at me when I try to talk to you?" or "Try to control your temper; the children shouldn't see me in tears every time you bark at me." The wife is now crying and the husband is reduced to exasperated, suppressed fury; he feels cheated of his anticipated sexual satisfaction and reproaches himself for his inability to control his anger, although he dimly feels that somehow he didn't start all this turmoil. He doesn't understand exactly what has happened, but he knows he has fallen into this trap dozens or hundreds of times before. Sexual intercourse between them is now emotionally impossible on this night, and the wife now can Decline the sexual advances she saw coming, which she did not want. She may cap the incident with tearful reproaches such as, "All you're interested in is my body; you don't care anything about me," or "I was feeling so affectionate toward you until you blew up at me and ruined it all," or "Every time I feel like getting close to you, you spoil it all somehow or other."

Certain aspects of this maneuver are worth considering in somewhat greater detail. It is, first of all, a put-off maneuver. It drives two people apart and threatens their interpersonal relationship. It occurs in the context of an emotionally charged relationship involving the wife's sexual frigidity, her husband's resentment about it, and, perhaps, a deteriorating marriage.

The actions of both persons are caused by emotional forces of which they are unaware. As she proceeds through the series of interpersonal acts which constitute the maneuver of Whine and Decline, she is not consciously aware that her actions are caused by her deeply rooted distaste for sexual intercourse. She believes in the reality of the maneuver she is executing. The husband also does not understand the maneuver in which he is involved; if he understood it, he would not be such a gullible and repeatedly disappointed participant.

The maneuver gives unhealthy emotional gratifications to one, or perhaps both, of the persons involved. Whine and Decline gives the wife the gratification of avoiding sexual activity which she finds distasteful. However, some women find still further satisfactions in this maneuver. Frustrating the husband's sexual desires may express a deeply rooted hostility toward men, especially when the husband's frustration is preceded by a certain amount of coy affection earlier in the evening which leads him on.

In occasional instances, the husband plays Whine and Decline with a readiness which thinly disguises gratifications he derives from the maneuver. For example, he may be seeking reasons to worsen a deteriorating marriage so he may seek more satisfactions outside it, and he may be laying the basis for a future divorce. He may find "scxual incompatibility" a ready reason to offer to himself and others to explain the dissolution of his marriage, or he may use Whine and Decline to convince himself of the necessity of extramarital affairs in which he engages from time to time.

Furthermore, the husband's readiness to engage in Whine and Decline occasionally arises from his own sexual difficulties such as premature ejaculations or partial impotence; he readily seizes upon his wife's provocations to quarrel and thus avoids sexual intercourse in which he fears he may not perform well.

The maneuver of Whine and Decline follows a basic pattern that is the same in all situations in which it is executed. Variations in technique occur, but they occur within the framework of the basic pattern. Both persons involved, however, are unaware, or only dimly aware, that they are employing a maneuver that is repetitive and predictable.

A stratagem differs from a maneuver in degree rather than in nature. A stratagem is more prolonged, more complex and more pervasive in its use by the person in his interpersonal relationships. Thus a stratagem may go on for years, decades or a lifetime. It usually is composed of a complex, diffusely employed set of acts woven together into an interpersonal pattern. It tends to be employed in many relationships rather than a single one. A person may use it in his relationship with his marital partner, his children and his relatives. In some instances, the person employs it in most social circles into which he ventures. Like maneuvers, stratagems are the expression of unconscious forces of which the person has little or no awareness, and he has superficial rationalizations to explain his behavior to himself and others. Also like maneuvers, the emotional releases achieved in stratagems are unhealthy ones, and the goals sought are interpersonally unsound. Once established in a person, a stratagem follows a pattern which is predictable and repetitive. Moreover, the same stratagems occur in many people, and, like maneuvers, they can be classified into groups and labeled with specific names. The nature of stratagems is best demonstrated by an example. A typical kind of stratagem is You Can Never Repay Me.

You Can Never Repay Me: A Stratagem

This stratagem is commonly employed by domineering mothers to control their children, who may range from five to fifty years in age. The mother makes, or claims to make, ostentatious sacrifices for the benefit of the child. She then uses these sacrifices to induce so profound a sense of obligation in the child that she can be repaid only by endless deference to her demands. The mother is skillful in using her real or alleged sacrifices to whip the child into line whenever he deviates from submission to her wishes, although this domination may be camouflaged behind a façade of whimpering resignation. At appropriate moments she lashes her child with such statements as "Go ahead and enjoy yourself; after all, your happiness is what I worked and slaved for all the years you were growing up and going through school," or "Old clothes are good enough for me; we brought you up accustomed to better things, but we can do without such luxuries." The mother usually begins this stratagem when the child is young, and by the time the child reaches adolescence the stratagem is so entrenched in the mother-child relationship that it often lasts until the mother's death releases the child from bondage. However, it may not stop even then, for the mother's death may leave a devastating turmoil in the child which may cause depression or other types of emotional difficulties.

Though it might not appear so at first glance, You Can Never Repay Me is a come-on type of stratagem. However, the forces which bind the mother and her children together are not love and reasonable devotion but guilt and a false sense of obligation.

As in all stratagems, the interpersonal goals of the strategist, the mother, are unhealthy. She is seeking to bind her children in a relationship of domination and submission rather than comfortable affection. The interpersonal results also are unhealthy, since the mother becomes a tyrant and children become her guilt-ridden servants. All parties involved in the stratagem are unaware of the emotional forces which motivate them. The mother believes in her role as the self-sacrificing martyr to whom obedient devotion is due, and the children have been so indoctrinated that they accept this concept and believe themselves bound to her by love rather than rasping guilt. Once established, You Can Never Repay Me lasts for decades or a lifetime, and its course is fairly predictable. It is a common stratagem and follows a similar pattern in each family in which it occurs.

In the following chapters we shall first consider the maneuvers and stratagems which occur within the family and then proceed to consider maneuvers and stratagems in broader relationships. On the whole, we shall spend more time considering stratagems than maneuvers, since stratagems have more decisive effects on the lives of people. As we proceed, the nature of the put-off and come-on forces which are woven into the maneuvers and stratagems will be apparent, and their disruptive or cohesive effects will be clear.

The most crucial maneuvers and stratagems usually are executed inside the family. They occur between parents and children, between husband and wife, between brothers and sisters, and sometimes between grandparents and grandchildren. Maneuvers and stratagems which occur outside the family usually have less drastic emotional impacts on the involved persons, although their economic, social and vocational influences may be great.

2

Maneuvers and Stratagems of Mothers with Children

A personality is gradually formed by the kinds of relationships the individual has with the important people in his life. This process begins in infancy and continues throughout life. However, the interpersonal relationships of childhood and early adolescence are crucial in laying down basic personality characteristics. The experiences of adulthood continue to affect emotional functioning, but their influence is less basic than the interpersonal environment the person had during his formative years. In a crude way, personality development may be likened to writing on a blackboard; the designs made during the formative years are made on an unmarked slate, but the marks made in adult life are being recorded on a slate already extensively filled with designs.

Hence, the most important factors in personality development are the individual's relationships with his mother, his father, his brothers and sisters, and other close persons. Interpersonal relationships at school, in the neighborhood, and in other broad social groups also play significant roles, but they are secondary to the more intense influences inside the family. Moreover, the maneuvers and stratagems a child experiences in his family life often determine the kinds of maneuvers and stratagems he will execute in adult life. As adults, most people tend to carry out stratagems, or variations of them, that they learned from their mothers and fathers.

The role of heredity in personality development and in determining the stratagems of people is much less than the influence of environment. To say that a person is hostile, just like his mother, does not necessarily mean that he inherited his hostility from her. It is more likely that the individual learned a lot of hostile maneuvers and stratagems from his mother while being reared by her.

To study the influence of human heredity on personality development by examining family histories is an unreliable process, because the investigator usually has to rely on hearsay reports about what grandparents and great-grandparents were like, and such reports have little scientific value; a psychiatrist must examine a person directly to get a valid appraisal of his personality and the kinds of maneuvers and stratagems he executes. To study heredity in rats, which produce a new generation once every several months or so, is much easier. A basic difficulty in studying heredity in humans is that the life-span of the investigator is the same as that of the subjects he is studying.

Thus we do not really know a great deal about how heredity influences personality, but most psychiatrists today feel that environment is much more important than heredity in determining personality structure and the stratagems a person uses.

A person's relationship with his mother during his childhood and early adolescence plays a large role in his personality development. In terms of hour-to-hour and day-to-day interaction, a child spends more time with his mother than with any other person during his formative years. Though other persons, especially the father, gradually assume large roles during the child's years of later childhood and adolescence, no one as a rule exceeds the mother in her influence. Hence, the kind of relationship the mother gives her child, the kinds of put-off and come-on forces that exist between them, and the kinds of maneuvers and stratagems she executes with him have a large impact.

Desirably, a mother should give her child much secure love and tenderness. The child who experiences comfortable love and security in his crucial relationships during his growing years will tend to look forward to later relationships with other people as satisfying and comfortable. On the other hand, the child who throughout his growing years is treated with rejection, anxiousness or hostility will tend in later years to be frightened of people, or rebellious and hostile toward them, or confused in his feelings about people and how he should interact with them. These influences begin to affect the person early in life; even an infant is sensitive in an inarticulate way to whether the persons caring for him are affectionate, anxious, hostile or rejecting. These influences continue throughout childhood and into adolescence as personality, in all its many facets, is formed.

A mother also should be able to impose the necessary limits on her child's behavior and occasionally to back these limitations up with reasonable discipline. She should be able to allow her child progressive independence in his late childhood and adolescence. Moreover, she sets a pattern for behavior in the family, in the neighborhood, and in broader social groups. Her relationship with her husband gives the child his earliest ideas about what goes on in a marriage. Everyone is an expert on one marriage, the marriage of his parents; though he may not be able to analyze that marriage consciously, it usually has much influence on his expectations and capacities in marriage when he is an adult.

We shall now examine some of the more common maneuvers and stratagems and put-off and come-on forces which occur in the relationships of mother and child. These stratagems usually begin during the child's early years and continue throughout his childhood and adolescence; often they persist in the mother-child relationship after the child has grown into adulthood. When a mother uses more than one stratagem with her child, one of them tends to predominate and to set the dominant theme of the mother-child relationship. Some mothers use small, unimportant maneuvers and stratagems once in a while, whereas others execute crucial, grim stratagems much of the time.

Queen Bee

In occasional families a bitter, competitive struggle arises between a mother and her daughter for the affection and attention of the father. Mothers who work this stratagem usually are immature, demanding women who cannot tolerate a female rival for the center of family attention. In such a family the mother and daughter engage in a rasping, chronic battle to see who will be Queen Bee. These mothers often adjust better to their sons; they may dominate them slightly, but they usually let them go their independent ways. These women frequently cling immaturely to their husbands, with whom they may get along reasonably well in a Baby Doll-Big Daddy way. However, the impact on the daughter of being caught in Queen Bee may be serious. Queen Bee is fueled by devastating put-off forces.

I recall an eighteen-year-old girl whose mother played a vicious stratagem of Queen Bee with her. The girl was the last of four children, and her three older siblings were boys. An interval of six years separated her from her youngest brother. Mother adjusted adequately to her sons; although she sometimes indulged them and at other times tried to dominate them, she was able to give them adequate love and to let them gradually acquire independence as they grew older. She tended to view them as young replicas of her husband, a successful, somewhat officious lawyer who was much impressed with his own importance. He treated his wife with the tolerant indulgence of a great man toward a charming, frivolous admirer. The roles of Baby Doll and Big Daddy met the personality needs of both wife and husband in this marriage and provided a setting in which their three sons could grow up without developing any striking personality problems. The daughter, however, besides being viewed unconsciously by the mother as female rival in the hive, was born at a time when the mother did not want another child and did not expect to have one. Thus, in addition to the hostility and depreciation which this girl was to experience in the stratagem of Queen Bee, she had the hazard of being an unwanted child.

The stratagem of Queen Bee began early, and Mother's hostility seeped out at every point. This child, she proclaimed, was a "difficult baby" who cried excessively, ate poorly and was not affectionate and cuddly as her older brothers had been. Mother found weaning and toilet training this child difficult because of the child's inherent "obstinacy" and "contrariness." Since Mother's hostility toward the child gradually produced the obstinacy which she described as part of the child's basic personality, Father in time accepted Mother's point of view. Moreover, since Father had not been annoyed by midnight crying and many petty troubles during the childhood of his three sons, he assumed that his wife was a capable mother and that his daughter was a difficult child. In addition, Father was not used to people giving him trouble. He viewed himself as the kind of man whose importance should be obvious to all and who should not be disturbed by such things as midnight howling by a fretful child.

As the result of Mother's stratagem of Queen Bee, Daughter was marked early in life as an inferior, difficult person. Father sighed and consigned this secondary type of creature to Mother's care, and he concentrated his supply of paternal interest on his sons. Her older brothers ignored the girl as a troublesome little sister who was clearly inferior to them. By the time she was ten years old, the girl felt profoundly inadequate, unloved and unlovable. Her clothing was plain, her hair was straight and stringy, and she lacked the sprightly vivacity of other girls. Mother remained the vivacious, girlish center of family attention, and Daughter was a sallow, thin, awkward wallflower.

A mother who plays Queen Bee rarely stops even when she has succeeded in her stratagem; the stratagem is so ingrained in the mother-daughter relationship that the mother continues it long after her unconscious objectives are gained. The rasping battle continues until the girl leaves home in late adolescence or early adulthood, and the sniping often continues even after that.

Daughter passed her childhood, puberty and adolescence in the acid drizzle of her mother's depreciation and criticism. Mother's belittling of her daughter often took the form of unanswerable questions ostensibly intended to help her daughter to correct her inadequacies. Mother's devastating questions followed the pattern of: "Why can't you be charming and talk well with people the way your brothers do? Why must you continually embarrass your father and me in public?" "Straighten your dress. Why can't you ever look neat and attractive? Don't your father and I spend enough money buying you clothes?" "Why can't you smile sweetly like other girls? Haven't your father and I given you every advantage?" Mother continually admonished Daughter not to fidget in public and not to behave as if she didn't know what to do with her hands. Thus it went on endlessly. Mother reigned as Queen Bee, and Daughter was tolerated as someone who could not be reformed despite every resource of maternal solicitude and paternal money.

The only area in which the girl achieved some success was her studies. She retreated into studiousness, and she attempted by scholastic excellence to secure the approval she had never received and for which she desperately longed. She took difficult courses in school and did well in them. Her mother depreciated these accomplishments and complained that Daughter was a "bookworm"; Mother frequently preached the need for a "well-rounded personality" and censured a "lopsided personality" in which intellectual achievements were gained at the expense of social grace and sound personality development. Father had long since ceased to pay much attention to his daughter and accepted Mother's verdicts.

The mother's brainwashing of her daughter from early childhood through adolescence left the girl with deep-seated convictions of inadequacy and inferiority. She had a strong depressive thread in her personality, and much unconscious hostility and yearnings for affection gnawed painfully inside her. She had little insight into her emotional turmoil and the unhealthy family relationships which had produced them. No one in her family circle had ever treated her as a worthwhile person, and she felt that the unanimous depreciation and indifference which her family felt toward her proved the basic rottenness of her personality. Moreover, her timidity and lack of self-confidence isolated her from interpersonal contacts outside the home which might have helped her to some extent to achieve a more realistic view of herself.

At the age of eighteen this girl went away to college, where she was shy with other girls and uncomfortable with boys. As she approached her midyear examinations in her freshman year, she was flooded with panic at the thought that she might fail. She could not concentrate on her studies, and her terror of failure was joined by a wave of severe depressiveness. She felt that her feelings of inferiority were about to receive complete confirmation in a scholastic disaster. She foresaw a disgraceful return home to the reproaches of her mother and her father's disgust and indifference. She felt so profoundly worthless that her life seemed a meaningless, painful process which had no value for her or anyone else. One Saturday night she threw herself from the fourth-floor window of her college dormitory to the pavement below.

Though badly injured, she survived this suicidal attempt. After recovery from her injuries she remained eight months in a psychiatric hospital and continued in out-patient psychotherapy for three years following her discharge. She never returned to her parents' home, but lived separately and continued her studies. Mother had the home and family to herself. Her stratagem of Queen Bee was preeminently successful.

Look What You Did to Our Child

In occasional families the child becomes a shuttlecock batted back and forth between his parents in their chronic marital struggles. Each parent relentlessly tries to prove that the other parent is ruining the child, and by their combined efforts they may jointly accomplish that objective. The father's angry cries of "You're spoiling him rotten" are countered by the mother's tearful reproaches that "Your meanness is driving him into juvenile delinquency." Unfortunately, both of them may be right. Each parent triumphantly points to whatever problems the child may have as products of the other parent's mistakes in rearing him. Each parent is so caught up in Look What You Did to Our Child that neither one takes a close look at what is really happening to him; the parents' interest is in their own struggle, not in its effects on the child. Both parents are swept along by strong put-off feelings toward each other, and, although they proclaim fervent come-on feelings toward their child, their feelings about him actually are mixtures of put-offs and come-ons. The parents usually have many other areas of marital wrangling, but their fights over the child have the most lasting effects since they affect the child's lifelong personality structure.

I recall an adolescent boy named Harold whose parents had been involved in a hard stratagem of Look What You Did to Our Child since his early years. A sister, who was seven years older than Harold, had escaped with relatively little damage from a light stratagem of Look What You Did to Our Child, and in late adolescence she fled from her parents' turbulent home into an early marriage with a young man who lived in a distant city. The parents' worsening marital problems had a much more drastic effect on Harold.

The stratagem of Look What You Did to Our Child began as soon as Harold was old enough to walk and talk a little. Father carped chronically on Mother's indulgence of Harold and complained that she was mollycoddling him. Mother countered by alleging that Father had never liked the child and that someone had to give him love since Father obviously had none to offer the boy. Father raged while Mother hovered tearfully over her "neglected" child. The dinner table was a constant battleground as Mother coaxed Harold to eat and Father threatened to haul him off to the bedroom for a sound spanking if he didn't "stop all this nonsense and eat." Harold dallied at his food, for even at a young age he sensed that his mother's tears paralyzed his father and his father's exasperated explosions only made his mother stick more tenaciously to whatever she was doing.

Like most children caught in Look What You Did to Our Child, Harold at about the age of three became adept at playing his parents off against each other. He learned how to flee to his mother with complaints of his father's meanness to get anything he wanted from his mother and to complain to his father about his mother's bossy possessiveness to wheedle any kind of privilege or liberty out of him. His mother cajoled and his father expostulated, but neither one gave him secure love or effective discipline. Harold was a thing to his parents rather than a person. He was a pawn in their marital struggles, and *what* he was was more important to them than *who* he was. Harold gradually grew into an indulged, demanding, self-centered child who dealt with people in sly, manipulative ways and was incapable of warm relationships with anybody.

The problems which Harold began to have in later childhood in the neighborhood and at school were seized upon by each parent as the result of the other parent's mismanagement of him. He was unruly at school, did badly in his studies, and got along poorly with other children in the neighborhood. Father triumphantly proclaimed these problems to be the result of Mother's indulgence, and Mother alleged that these problems were a spreading rebellion against Father's harshness. Both parents, moreover, had read enough laymen's books on psychiatry to be able to throw diagnoses back and forth at each other. Mother called Father a "rejecting parent," and Father labeled his wife an "overprotective mother." Father said Harold suffered from a bad case of "Momism," and Mother said Harold's troubles arose from "rebellion against a hostile, punitive father figure." Mother said Father needed a psychiatrist, and Father returned the remark to her; on this point they were both correct.

Harold slipped through childhood without any serious behavior problems at school or in the neighborhood, but ominous clouds appeared on the horizon as adolescence approached. Harold's self-centered demandingness and inability to tolerate frustration of his wishes left him ill equipped to adjust to the normal stresses of adolescence. Moreover, he was not capable of warm relationships with people, but tended to play them off against each other in sly, provocative ways. The first major blow to his parents came when Harold's despairing religious teachers reported that he had not learned enough to have his bar mitzvah at thirteen, and Harold refused to go on with further religious instruction. He contemptuously declared that he was "through with all that junk." His failure to go through with this religious confirmation jolted his parents, for it suddenly exposed Harold's behavior problems to the scrutiny of their relatives and friends. However, both parents had too long been entrenched in the stratagem of Look What You Did to Our Child to be able at this late stage to modify their behavior toward the boy or toward each other. Harold's increasing difficulties in adolescence only embittered his parents' struggle, and each new problem gave his parents new ammunition to fire back and forth at each other.

Harold soon was in trouble at high school because of arrogance to teachers, smoking in school corridors, fighting and truancy. He drove the family car without permission or a license, and the second time the police caught him he was given a suspended sentence by the juvenile court. He was expelled several times from high school for brief periods, and he refused to continue school after the age of sixteen. He got a job working nights in a drive-in restaurant, and his social group consisted of high-school dropouts and sexually promiscuous teenage girls. During his adolescence his parents made three attempts to get psychiatric help for him. In each instance, Harold refused to keep appointments or sparred with the psychiatrist with evasive comments and arrogant silence. Attempts to engage the parents in counseling resulted only in their chronic recrimination of each other, whether they were seen individually or in joint sessions; each one carried Look What You Did to Our Child into psychotherapy.

When Harold was nineteen he married a girl who was five months pregnant by him, and, being without a job and poorly educated, he turned to his parents for financial aid. His parents could not refuse to help their son and their expected grandchild, but the pattern of turning to his parents for financial aid threatened ominously to become chronic. The stratagem of Look What You Did to Our Child was over. It was time to pay the bill.

Torture Rack

In a stratagem of Torture Rack a mother deftly uses medical problems to dominate her children and other people around her. Any kinds of symptoms or diseases may be used, and the physical problem may be mild or severe. Torture Rack players may use even minor symptoms to dominate their families for decades. I recall a determined little woman who ruled her family for thirty years by the adept use of headaches. The least frustration of her wishes precipitated a headache, whereupon she lay on her bed with a wet washrag on her forehead and a grimace of agony on her face. Anyone who was not quickly quelled by this maneuver was speedily whipped into line by her groans and her repeated requests of

35

"Don't let my suffering change your plans; go ahead and do what you want to do."

A mother may use this stratagem with small children, adolescents and adult sons and daughters, and occasionally it is employed to crush a husband into docile obedience. I have known women who ruled whole clans from beds of suffering. In this stratagem a bed becomes the equivalent of a medieval torture rack. The difference, however, is that in the modern stratagem of Torture Rack the apparent victim controls the wheels that increase or diminish her pain, and she twists or releases them depending on how recalcitrant or docile her children are at the moment. The victim triumphs over her victims. Torture Rack is a come-on type of stratagem which binds the children to the mother by feelings of guilt and a corrupted sense of obligation. Occasionally the stratagem backfires and the child rebels; then Torture Rack becomes a put-off stratagem.

Physical diseases which the strategist has may be exploited in Torture Rack; common diseases used are arthritis, cardiac disease, chronic lung disorders, low back orthopedic problems and headaches. Psychosomatic illnesses, in which emotional factors cause physical disorders, may be employed; these disorders include colitis, peptic ulcer, ulcerlike upper gastrointestinal difficulties, nausea, vomiting and others. Hysterical symptoms such as muscular paralyses, pains in many parts of the body, numbness and fainting may be used in Torture Rack. Both physically caused illnesses and emotionally caused dysfunctions may be employed concurrently.

Sometimes a Torture Rack strategist shops from doctor to doctor until she deceives one of them into operating on her. She then suffers for years or decades from "complications" of the operation such as "adhesions," "internal scars" and "post-operative pains." The children unhappily report to relatives and friends that "Mother has never been the same since she had her appendix out" or that "Mother has had pain every day of her life since they removed her left ovary." An occasional Torture Rack player may vomit and groan until she convinces a discouraged surgeon to operate once or twice more looking for pathology to explain so much misery. Such operations give Mother a powerful lever in her Torture Rack stratagem. Perceptive children may in time see through the use of headaches and stomachaches in Torture Rack, but surgical operations and their subsequent agony cannot be so easily swept aside.

Torture Rack involves two basic steps: (1) the disease, or diseases, must be established, and (2) exacerbations of the disease must be clearly linked to stresses caused by the disobedience or independence of the children. Once these two points are established, Mother is set to play Torture Rack for months, years or decades. Needless to say, the husband usually is included as one of the victims, but we are now examining only its effects on the children.

The terminology of Torture Rack shifts with new developments in medical science. For example, thirty years ago a Torture Rack strategist might have suffered from "nervousness" or "nervous exhaustion." Such terms are being abandoned by today's Torture Rack strategists, who have "depression," "anxiety" and other modernly phrased difficulties culled from television programs or from the dozens of books written each year to explain psychiatry to a bewildered public. I have seen a few sophisticated Torture Rack players who used "alcoholism" as a disease in this stratagem. These ladies explained to their families that to condemn alcoholism as a moral problem is a cruel injustice since modern medicine has demonstrated (which is true) that alcoholism is a disease which merits professional assistance and helpful understanding by the family. These ladies untiringly allege that the stressful behavior of their children and husbands is causing their troubles with the disease of alcoholism. The old cry "You drove me to drink" is gradually being replaced by the suburban wail "You made me sick."

The modern role of the hospital as "the doctor's workshop" has changed some of the rules of Torture Rack. This stratagem used to be worked mainly in the home with house calls by the doctor and continuous attention by the hovering family. Today this scene often is transferred to a hospital room where the strategist goes through batteries of tests and endless poking and probing. Exacerbations of symptoms predictably occur when relatives fail to decorate the bedside during visiting hours to listen to the details of the day's laboratory tests, X-rays, nurses' indifference, interns' errors and physicians' negligence. These women usually have veins that are difficult to puncture, and their incidence of vague, miserable side reactions to new medications is extraordinarily high. Widespread hospitalization insurance provides Torture Rack strategists with a new maneuver. Any small rebellion or independent gesture by a dominated child or a restless husband threatens to precipitate another ten-day stay in the hospital. "Whatever you do, don't upset Mother and cause her to go back to the hospital" becomes an established principle of family life.

Torture Rack strategists customarily divide their children into two categories, the "good children" and the "bad children." The "good children" are those who become homebound nurses and sympathizers to their chronically ill mothers; they receive scant praise and are plagued with lashing complaints whenever they falter in their duties. The "bad children" are those who free themselves and lead normal lives; they are chronically castigated *in absentia* for their cruel indifference to their suffering mothers, and Mother ominously hopes that "their children will never treat them as they have treated me."

Torture Rack may begin when the children are very small, or it may begin when they are in later childhood or adolescence. It often begins early; chains are more easily fastened on the young than on the grown. A mother who begins Torture Rack early characteristically lashes her children with "You're making me sick and driving me to an early grave," and "My sick headache is because of the disobedience and meanness of you and your brother," and "Can't you even behave when I am deathly sick and struggling to stay on my feet to make your meals and keep this home running for you?" Of course, many mothers make small maneuvers of Torture Rack once in a while in struggling to rear their children. These occasional lapses do no harm, but the daily impact of a hard stratagem of Torture Rack gradually corrupts the home. As the years go by, Torture Rack often causes increasingly serious damage to both the children and the mother. The mother becomes entrenched in her role and she sinks gradually into invalidism or semi-invalidism. The children are plagued with hostility and guilt feelings, both unconscious and conscious, toward the mother who has distorted their lives. They have been pounded for years or decades with the idea that the mother's health and perhaps even her life depend on how they behave toward her; when they dare to doubt the truth of this concept they are flooded with anxiousness and guilt. The end of Torture Rack often is played out between a peevish, invalided, aged mother and guilt-ridden, depressed, middle-aged children.

An old medical adage states that all hypochondriacs eventually die, but they never die of hypochondriasis. The stratagem of Torture Rack ends similarly. Mother eventually dies, but she rarely dies of one of the diseases she used to dominate her children. After her death her children are freed from her day-to-day demands, but the long grinding of submission and repressed anger and guilt often produce emotional turmoil in the children for months or years.

However, Torture Rack does not always end so grimly. Family physicians, internists and psychiatrists frequently can break up the stratagem, at least for the children, by helping them gain some insight into it. The beginning of the end of Torture Rack may come when a physician says, "Look, your mother's problems have a big emotional overlay, and, moreover, she is using these symptoms to run all of you ragged and to dominate you. This is merely making you miserable and getting her deeper into the rut of a medical invalid. Free yourself from all this, and do both yourself and her a favor."

No Maneuvers or Stratagems at All

In Chapter 1 we specified that, by definition, maneuvers and stratagems are unhealthy interpersonal operations. Desirably, a mother should give her child love and acceptance and also should not execute any maneuvers or stratagems with him. However, to ignore a child completely, giving him neither love and acceptance nor maneuvers and stratagems, is even more devastating. The most destructive put-off stratagem a mother can play with her child is No Maneuvers or Stratagems at All. In this stratagem the mother refuses to become involved with the child; she becomes a non-mother and treats him as a nonchild. She does not treat the child with hostility, or anxiousness, or possessiveness, or domination, or love and acceptance. She arranges her life so that the child's basic physical needs are met by other people, and she continues her own activities with bland indifference to the child. Complete emotional rejection of a child can be more devastating than rasping hostility; unhealthy interaction with a difficult mother is sometimes better than the aching vacuum of no interaction at all.

In No Maneuvers or Stratagems at All the child receives minimal attention from his mother during the early weeks and months of his life. Mother consigns the child to the impersonal coldness of a stream of babysitters, day-nursery attendants and household maids. She resolves the annoyance of the child's crying by closing the doors which separate his bedroom from her own. Feeding and diapering become mechanical procedures which are carried out without love and often are assigned to whoever happens to be available at the moment; the child often lies soiled or hungry for hours before his needs are met. In time the infant often becomes apathetic, withdrawn, fretful and thin. His lusty cries degenerate into whining whimpers. He hangs limp in the arms of an attendant, passively lets himself be handled like a sack of flour, and does not respond with cuddling warmth to the few physical contacts he has with people. He eats poorly, his growth lags, and he is susceptible to illnesses. Just as plants need the stimulus of sun and rain, children need the tenderness of an affectionate mother. Even the irritable care of a hostile mother stimulates more interpersonal vivacity and growth than the vacuum of maternal indifference.

As the child grows older he may be left alone for long periods of time or consigned to the negligent care of a busy maid or a telephone-bound teenage babysitter. Often he is a withdrawn, shy child who makes few demands on people around him, and his apathy makes it easy for those caring for him to ignore him. Even people who try to reach him emotionally find it hard to do so; he shrinks from interpersonal relationships, since in his experience he has found them only a painful vacuum. At school he is withdrawn from the crowd, and neighbors find him a "strange, cold little fellow."

No Maneuvers or Stratagems at All may occur in any socioeconomic group. It may be carried out by working mothers whose days are filled with work at the office and whose evenings and weekends are filled with bowling leagues, weekend party groups, card parties and so forth. This stratagem may be executed by professional-class people whose lives are filled with professional work, committee meetings, cocktail parties, out-of-town travel, country-club parties and all the other paraphernalia of affluent suburban life. A well-to-do mother may consign her child to servants who change every few months, and the mother has only brief contacts with the child as she prepares to go out for dinner.

The devastating effects of No Maneuvers or Stratagems at All may be diminished if the child's needs for maternal affection are met by relatives, affectionate babysitters, neighbors or whoever else takes a sympathetic interest in him. However, even though he receives some affection from other mother figures, the indifference of his own mother has a special impact on him. No Maneuvers or Stratagems at All often leaves the child with feelings of worthlessness, isolation and aching hunger for closeness with a protecting person. Such feelings often persist into adult life and affect the person's relationships at work, in marriage and in social groups. He goes through life groping for the maternal love he never had, but he does not know what he is looking for or why he searches so restlessly for it.

In other instances, the child who is involved in No Maneuvers or Stratagems at All is diffusely angry at a world which has not met his emotional needs. He feels bitter rebellion and a detachment from people. His hostility seeps out in his relationships with both men and women; he is an irritable marital partner and an impatient parent. He is prone to execute some variation of No Maneuvers or Stratagems at All with his own children, and so the web of unhealthy interpersonal relationships is spun from one generation to another.

No Maneuvers or Stratagems at All sometimes is softened by the attentions of a father who attempts to fill the gap left by the mother's uninvolvement with the child. This may be a partial help, but many of the child's emotional needs still go unmet. The grimmest form of No Maneuvers or Stratagems at All occurs when both parents play it with a child; the child does not impinge on either of their lives in a significant way. Often such children are lost in the shuffle of their parents' divorces, alcoholism, extramarital affairs, vocational absorptions and social activities. I recall a ten-year-old girl who was involved in a double stratagem of No Maneuvers or Stratagems at All. Her father was a businessman for whom home was merely a base of operations where he changed clothing, ate occasional meals and slept when he was in town. Her mother lived in a world of morning committee meetings, organizational lunches, afternoon bridge parties, late afternoon cocktail parties and endless dinners out in the evening. Their daughter wandered through childhood in the empty corridors of parental neglect. When she was ten her desolation, depressiveness and unconscious fury erupted in a case of anorexia nervosa, a psychosomatic illness in which the child cannot eat and becomes dangerously emaciated, and this illness abruptly concentrated her parents' attention on her for the first time in her life.

As a rule, there is no clear end point to No Maneuvers or Stratagems at All; the child wanders aimlessly until late adolescence, and then he slowly straggles out into the world. In many cases its legacy is the long stratagem of No Maneuvers or Stratagems at All which the person plays in all the interpersonal relationships of his life throughout his adult years.

3

Maneuvers and Stratagems
of Fathers with Children

During the first year or so of life, a child's relationship with his mother is the most important facet of his interpersonal life. After that, the father gradually assumes a role equal to the mother's in the child's interpersonal world. The kind of relationship a child has with his father and the kinds of stratagems the father plays with him have a large effect on the child's personality development.

Even during the child's infancy, the father, through his relationship with the mother, has a significant impact on the emotional atmosphere in which the child is raised. The father who gives his wife a comfortable, secure relationship in their marriage helps the mother provide the child with a tender mother-child relationship. However, when the father's behavior leaves the mother chronically anxious, insecure or angry, he may prevent her from settling down in a comfortable relationship with the child.

As the child grows older, his father's direct interpersonal life with him has an increasing impact on his personality development. A boy should find affection, firmness and comradeship in his father; a girl should find the same qualities, although her interests and activities usually are more closely tied to those of her mother. However, when a father is hostile and rejecting to his children, or when he is so passive or indecisive that he cannot set reasonable

45

limits on their behavior, the children may develop unhealthy personality features. Personality problems are especially prone to occur in a child when both the father-child and the mother-child relationships are defective. Multiple stratagems usually are more devastating than single stratagems.

The emotional process called "identification" is an important facet of personality development. A boy who has a healthy relationship with his father gradually assumes many of the attitudes and characteristics of his father. This process, which is largely unconscious, has much influence on the boy's development of masculine interests and his concepts of desirable social and ethical behavior. In a similar way, a girl with a healthy relationship with her mother assumes her mother's feminine orientations and qualities. However, when the child's relationship with his parent of the same sex is unhealthy, the child's identification with him may be distorted or incomplete. Distorted or incomplete identification may have grave effects on the person's sexual orientation and his capacities for successful interpersonal living both in intimate relationships and in broader social groups.

In some instances, the stratagems that fathers and mothers play with children cause distortions of sexual identification. For example, a boy with a possessive, domineering mother and a passive, ineffectual father may identify primarily with his mother; such an identification may lead to homosexuality or other kinds of sexual problems. In a similar way, a girl may become homosexual or develop other sexual problems when unhealthy relationships with her parents prevent identification with her mother and cast her into a distorted identification with her father.

An important aspect of being a healthy parent is allowing a child the gradual independence he must assume during late childhood and adolescence as he slowly grows toward adulthood. Some fathers and mothers cling too much to their children, whereas others cast them off too early. Some parents cannot accept the increasing individuality, the sexual maturation and the evolving independence of their children who are, step by step, becoming adults.

We shall now consider some of the more common maneuvers and stratagems fathers may carry out with their children. These stratagems often begin during the child's early years, but they may start in his late childhood or adolescence. They frequently continue to color the father-child relationship after the child has reached adulthood.

All Boys Are Lecherous

All Boys Are Lecherous is played occasionally between fathers and their adolescent daughters. This stratagem is precipitated by unconscious sexual stirrings aroused in a father by living in the same household with his sexually attractive adolescent daughter. Father resolves these unacceptable rumblings toward his daughter by becoming the vigilant protector of her virginity against the hordes of adolescent boys and young men whom he accuses of lecherous designs upon her. At times the father's turmoil erupts in angry accusations toward his daughter when she refuses to abide by the restrictions he puts on her dating. All Boys Are Lecherous is fueled by come-on feelings of the father toward his daughter, but the end result sometimes is a brief or long-lasting put-off rupture between them.

The stratagem of All Boys Are Lecherous may take various forms. I recall an eighteen-year-old girl's father who chased off all his daughter's admirers by his incessant "practical jokes." One of his favorite practical jokes was to smear hair oil and shaving cream over the steering wheel, seats, gearshift and door handles of the car of each boy who came to call on his daughter or to take her out on a date. He professed innocent amazement that his little jokes drove the boys off and reduced his daughter to tears. He said that modern boys simply didn't have the rough-and-ready sense of humor that young men had during his own youth. By such maneuvers he quashed his daughter's dating and restricted her social life. He said it was just as well that she didn't date much since "all boys nowadays are only interested in sex and are no good." After attending junior college for two years while living at home, the girl managed to escape to an out-of-town college where she began to date with greater freedom. Father continued to criticize each young man she dated at college, whether he had met him or not. When his daughter became engaged to a medical student, Father prophesied that his daughter would suffer much marital misery because of her husband's neglect while working the proverbially long hours of a physician. To his great disappointment, the doctor became an anesthesiologist in a large medical group and was home most evenings.

In some instances All Boys Are Lecherous leads to severe turmoil in the home. This is especially true when there is no blood bond between the father and his adolescent daughter—when, for example, the girl is the child of the mother by a previous marriage. This situation is becoming more common in our society with the increased incidence of divorce. Especially if the girl's true father takes little interest in her or is deceased, the turmoil of All Boys Are Lecherous becomes intense as the foster father's unconscious sexual attraction to the girl causes him to become indignant and crudely accusatory.

I recall a forty-two-year-old man who demanded that his sixteen-year-old foster daughter should not date at all. He said that all boys were bums and that girls could not be trusted in their skillfully seductive, lecherous company; he stated that his daughter would be "like putty in their hands." For a couple of years he prevented her from dating, but when she was eighteen she began to date with the quiet encouragement of her mother, who saw the girl's social development suffering under the foster father's restrictions. When the girl started dating, the father's accusations against her and her boyfriends became crude and constant. He demanded that the mother search the girl's underwear for signs of sexual activity and that she look for grass stains on the girl's skirts. His glaring hostility toward the boys she dated embarrassed the family, and she began to meet her dates at the homes of friends. Father stated that this was conclusive evidence of her sexual delinquency and said that if she had nothing to hide she would have the boys come to their home. He waited up until she came home from dates, ranted at her and sometimes called her a "tramp" and a "whore."

The father's marital relationship with the girl's mother deteriorated and he accused his wife of encouraging her daughter's sexual delinquency. The sexual relationship of the mother and father deteriorated and they seldom had intercourse. Finally, when the girl was twenty she eloped with a young medical corpsman in the Navy and established a home of her own in a distant town near the naval base at which her husband was stationed. After the girl left home, All Boys Are Lecherous ended. With some grumbling, Father accepted the young man, who came from a family in their own neighborhood. In time he became cordial to his foster daughter and her husband, and his marital relationship with his wife improved markedly. Fortunately, the mother's other two children by her first marriage were boys, and so the family had to go through All Boys Are Lecherous only once.

The stratagem of All Boys Are Lecherous usually ends, or at least diminishes in intensity, when the girl marries or leaves home to work in a distant city. In most instances it does not leave a lasting mark on the girl's life, since the father-daughter relationship may have been good until the girl's middle adolescence. However, in occasional instances the painful turmoil of All Boys Are Lecherous drives the girl into an unwise early marriage to get out of the home. When a girl desperately flees an unhappy home to enter a hasty marriage, she is prone to make an unwise choice; her resulting marital misery may give the father ample opportunity to preach, "I told you so. All that boy was interested in was your body. As soon as the newness of that wore off, he showed himself to be the irresponsible bum I always said he was. Maybe you and your mother will listen to me next time." In this way the father who plays All Boys Are Lecherous may contribute to causing some of the problems he prophesies.

In All Boys Are Lecherous the actions of the father are caused by unconscious emotional forces which neither he nor his daughter understands. In an unhealthy way, All Boys Are Lecherous resolves the father's unconscious sexual attraction toward his daughter and gives it a distorted expression in a stratagem of this basic pattern.

That Awful Woman

In That Awful Woman the father plays the children and the mother off against each other in ways that depreciate the mother and alienate the children from her; these manipulations enable the father to control the entire family. The father has strong put-off feelings toward both his wife and his children, but he camouflages them with protestations of much come-on devotion. This stratagem is not as common as the previous ones we have discussed, but it demonstrates how one person's interpersonal stratagem may devastate an entire family.

That Awful Woman usually begins with maneuvers in which the father precipitates chronic marital discord by subtly stabbing his wife in her sensitive areas. After the mother has been reduced to fits of screaming anger and chronic irritability toward both her husband and the children, the father turns to the children with despairing innocence and says, "What can anyone do with such an impossible woman? Nothing I do pleases her. Her ranting and raving is making us all miserable. Let's get out of here for a few hours until she calms down and comes to her senses." The unconscious force in the father which propels him into these maneuvers often is a deep-seated hostility toward women which arose during painful experiences with his mother in his own childhood. His hostility toward women in general focuses most intensely on his wife.

In other instances, the hostility of a man who plays That Awful Woman arises from homosexuality. His homosexual problems may be latent and unconscious, or he may have followed an overt homosexual pattern both before marriage and during it. A homosexual man has much hostility toward women beneath the façade of urbane charm with which he may treat them socially. At least half of all homosexual men marry at some time during their lives, but their marriages often are chaotic and frequently end in divorce.

The children are the major victims of That Awful Woman, though the wife also suffers much. The children are reared by an irritable, haggard mother and a cold, manipulative father. Caught in a cruel stratagem they cannot understand and utterly unaware of the true personalities of both their parents, the children may develop marked personality problems; however, sometimes they survive in better shape than would be expected.

I recall a twenty-two-year-old girl who was the product of a lifelong stratagem of That Awful Woman. Her father was a cold, unscrupulous merchant who had made much money by exploiting his business associates and his customers. His behavior both in business and in social relationships varied between smiling persuasiveness and angry bullying, depending on which role best suited his aims of the moment. His behavior in his marriage was alternately persuasive and hostile; two children were born into this marriage, and the older of them was my patient.

The father's stratagem of That Awful Woman began during my patient's early childhood. He nagged the mother unmercifully about each small failing she had and justified his behavior by saying that he was only trying to help her improve so that she could "give a better home to our children." A few years of such torture reduced the mother to chronic irritability and erratic fits of anger. Thus the father worked out the initial maneuvers of That Awful Woman and he was ready for the main part of the stratagem. He assumed the role of the calm, reasonable parent who was trying to save the children from the screaming rage and floundering inadequacies of That Awful Woman. He referred to their home as "that hellhole" and often took the children to his store, or to his sister's home, or on weekend trips to "get them away from *that awful woman.*" These separations further disturbed the mother, who saw her behavior driving the children away from her but, under the father's incessant jabbing, was unable to alter it.

When my patient was fourteen her mother died of carcinoma of the breast after a two-year illness. Her mother's death left the girl with much unresolved anger toward her mother and devastating guilt about her feelings. She confusedly sensed that both she and her mother had suffered much, but beyond this point she could see no further. When the girl was sixteen her father remarried; his second wife was an immature, emotionally unstable woman who brought a child by a previous marriage into the home. Within a year the old stratagem began again, involving his children and That Awful Woman, their stepmother. At eighteen the girl went away to college in a distant city and thus escaped from the vicious stratagems in which she had been involved all her life. When her graduation from college drew near four years later and she faced the prospect of returning to her home city and her father's house, she became very upset and sought psychiatric help. In time psychotherapy freed her permanently from the stratagem which had distorted her life; she understood the personalities of her mother, her father and her stepmother, and she resolved the hostility, guilt and unmet yearnings for affection she felt toward all three of them.

The same stratagem, of course, can be played by a woman against her husband, and then it is called That Awful Man. A frequent theme in That Awful Man is the alleged or actual marital infidelity of the husband and his consequent neglect of the children and the home. The story of the father's extramarital excursions may be true, or exaggerated, or fictitious, but the impact of it on the children is the same. In some instances, the oft-cited episode of infidelity was a brief peccadillo which the mother exaggerates into a chronic issue with daily hammering on it for years or decades. In other instances, the mother's sexual coldness and nagging drive the father to seek extramarital solace. Having executed this maneuver, the mother then begins the main stratagem of That Awful Man. The histrionic screaming and threats of suicide which may accompany That Awful Man may exceed the melodramatic misery portrayed on television serials. Often the truth is grimmer than fiction.

I'll Take Over Later

I'll Take Over Later is a put-off stratagem which a rejecting father may carry out with his son. The father's theme is: "I'll let his mother raise him during his younger years, and I'll take over when he's old enough to do things with me." The father may speculate vaguely that the boy will arrive at the age of "taking over" when he is ready to go hunting and fishing, to attend football games, to go on trips with him, and so forth. The father usually postpones the age of comradeship from one year to the next throughout his son's childhood and adolescence. I'll Take Over Later camouflages the father's put-off rejection of his son and his indifference to him.

In some instances the father who executes this stratagem takes a few steps toward forming a relationship with his son when the boy is in late childhood or adolescence. He may then discover that the gulf which has widened between himself and his son is so vast that it cannot be bridged. When he gets ready to "take over" his son, he may encounter something he hadn't expected; the boy must be willing to be taken over, and often he is indifferent to his father's approaches. He avoids his father's overtures, and their interests are so different that no bonds can be formed. The father may dismiss his failure to reach the boy by saying that the right time to take over obviously has not yet arrived, and the oft-promised take-over is delayed another year or two. In the end, I'll Take Over Later becomes I'll Take Over Never.

In some instances, the boy has sharp resentment, which may be conscious or unconscious, about his father's rejection of him. In other cases an empty vacuum with neither hostility nor affection occurs between father and son. Occasionally, the boy drifts into an unhealthy closeness with his mother and perhaps an identification with her. I recall a seventeen-year-old boy whose father was horrified to find that when he wanted to take his son on weekend hunting trips the boy was interested mainly in ballet lessons and boyfriends with similar interests. The father winced at his son's apparent effeminacy but reassured himself that "the kid will grow out of it." Unfortunately, the boy's slowly evolving homosexual pattern was a painful retribution to the father for the neglect of his son.

How well the boy turns out frequently depends on the personality soundness of the mother who must really "take over" during the boy's formative years. Some wise mothers steer their sons into activities with substitute father figures in scout work, boys' athletic groups, school activities, well-run summer camps, and so forth. Such boys may emerge from a long hard stratagem of I'll Take Over Later in reasonably good condition. However, in other instances the mother fills the gap by possessive overprotectiveness of the boy. Rejected by his father and falling into a close come-on relationship with an engulfing mother, the boy in occasional instances identifies with the mother and gradually assumes her attitudes and orientations. He may become effeminate and fastidious in manner but maintain a heterosexual orientation in his sexual impulses; he may, however, develop overt homosexual problems. When the father finally gets around to "taking over," he may discover that he has lost his son, and he finds an effeminate stranger in his place.

Sometimes a business or professional man justifies his long neglect of his son by saying that he is busy building a family business or a professional practice for his son to join and take over someday. It would be far better for the father to spend more time with the boy during his formative years so that the boy could develop the personality structure and interests which would enable him to join his father in his vocational activities in later years. Modern urban life makes I'll Take Over Later an easy stratagem to use. The endless treadmill of business activities, entertaining customers, cocktail parties, attending committee meetings and conventions, out-of-town travel and so forth can so clutter a man's life that a mild inclination to employ I'll Take Over Later can easily become the dominant theme in a man's relationship with his son.

In the early years of my practice I occasionally tried the melodramatic gesture of writing on a prescription pad, "Rx: Spend one hour each day with your son and take a double dose on weekends." The prescriptions rarely were filled and I stopped writing them. To date, we still do not have a simple prescription for I'll Take Over Later.

Sledge Hammer

The stratagem of Sledge Hammer is carried out by domineering, tyrannical fathers who have profound emotional needs to control the people around them. They bully, belittle and rant at their wives and children and pound them into submission, evasiveness or chaotic rebellion. The man who plays Sledge Hammer often is married to a passive woman who can neither resist his bullying nor remove herself and the children from the home. Though it might at first appear to be a put-off stratagem, Sledge Hammer actually is motivated by come-on forces in the father. He tries to use rasping domination to bind his children to him, but the end result often is an explosive put-off rupture.

The turmoil which goes on in a Sledge Hammer family may

not be apparent to the outside world. I recall a suburban lady who summarized the atmosphere of their home when she said, "Doctor, on the same day my husband and I went to the American Legion post to receive the annual award as the ideal family, we had been up until two o'clock in the morning arguing and fighting. As a matter of fact I had to put extra makeup on my face to hide the black eye my husband gave me." Less than two years after they received this "ideal family" award, their teenage daughter became illegitimately pregnant, their son was a college dropout, and the husband was threatened with indictment for income-tax fraud. Sledge Hammer may be played behind a façade of Home Sweet Home.

Frequently men who play Sledge Hammer unconsciously choose passive, floundering women as their mates. They marry women who will be too passive to fight back against their ranting tyranny and too frightened of the outside world to be able to extricate themselves from the miserable marriages into which they have fallen. Before marriage, the woman interprets the man's domineering qualities as "strength of character" and "firmness," and she feels she will find shelter and protection in marriage with him. After marriage she discovers that she mistook brutality and tyranny for strength. However, the stratagem of Sledge Hammer by then has begun, and often it lasts until "death do you part."

The impact of Sledge Hammer descends heavily upon the children. They are reared in the hailstorm of their father's tirades and the mist of their mother's tears. As the father rages, the mother whimpers. The children grow up with confused feelings of anger, guilt and inferiority. They are angry, either consciously or unconsciously, toward their father for his brutality and toward their mother for her inability to remove them from their intolerable home. The children may emerge from this environment as passive, frightened persons with psychoneurotic or psychosomatic problems, or they may erupt during adolescence into chaotic rebellion against the father. The boys who come from such homes sometimes are candidates to start new stratagems of Sledge Hammer in their own marriages, and the problems of one generation are propagated into the next.

I recall an adolescent boy whose father had played a hard stratagem of Sledge Hammer with him all his life. The boy was a beaten, passive, awkward teenager who did poorly in school despite good intelligence. When he was seventeen his repressed hostility against his father began to seep out in a devastating way. He began to forge checks for small amounts in his father's name on banks in which his father did not have accounts. The father was a government bank examiner, and the banks understandably were anxious not to alienate him. Each time a forged check appeared the bank merely called the father to report that another one of his son's checks had arrived, and the humiliated father rushed to the bank to make it good. He then returned home to rant for a couple of hours at his son, who sat glumly and stared at the floor. The boy cashed these checks at the rate of one each week for two years and finally gave up this stratagem. I later saw him in his early twenties for a severe obsessive compulsive psychoneurosis.

The father's hostility usually is verbal only, though occasionally it may spill over into slaps and blows. However, the effects of a blow usually disappear with fading of the bruise it causes, but words may leave lifelong injuries. The major blows in Sledge Hammer consist of torrents of depreciation and guilt-slinging. A typical harangue is: "Why was I ever burdened with a lazy, stupid, good-for-nothing son like you? What have I done to deserve a family like this? Can't you ever do anything right? Don't hide behind your mother's skirts. Stand up and face me like a man; at least do that, even if you can't do anything else." Skillful Sledge Hammer strategists can continue such tirades of depreciation, guilt and hostility for hours at a time. The dinner table is a favorite place for such explosions because the family is gathered together and the children can be humiliated before each other. Moreover, at dinner the family is more or less a captive audience since no one dares to leave before dessert is over.

A favorite tactic of a Sledge Hammer father is to propound an unanswerable question and to follow it with an endless harangue. An example of an unanswerable question is: "Why do you do what you do? Just explain it to me. I want to know. Why do you do all these things all the time?" The child or adolescent does not understand why he does what he does and probably could not put it into words even if he did know. Another favorite unanswerable question is: "What kind of person are you to do things like that? Don't you ever stop to think? What kind of person are you anyway?" Only a psychiatrist could answer a question like that, and his explanation of what the child was like and who made him that way would not please the father.

Sometimes a hostile father carries out a more subtle stratagem than outright Sledge Hammer. Instead of banging away with crude blows, he stabs with sharp, quick thrusts. His stilettos are the sarcastic comment, the ironic question, the pitying sneer and the hopeless sigh of resignation at the utter inadequacies of his children. This variant of Sledge Hammer may be labeled Ice Pick; often, it is the worse of the two.

Tandem Paternity

During the past forty years the rising divorce rate has created a common new phenomenon, Tandem Paternity. About twenty-five percent of all American marriages now end in divorce, and since the children usually stay with the mother and the majority of divorced mothers remarry, between ten and twenty percent of all children now have more than one father during their formative years. For want of a better name, we shall call this Tandem Paternity.

Tandem Paternity is not a stratagem; it is a new kind of arena. It creates possibilities for new maneuvers and stratagems and new combinations of them. It is as if the conventional baseball diamond were abandoned and a six-sided infield with six bases were laid out in its place, or as if the conventional rectangular football field were discarded and a circular field with four sets of goal posts were constructed. New maneuvers and stratagems could be executed on such playing fields, and a certain amount of confusion would be inevitable.

The change in fathers may be for the better or the worse in its effect on the child's personality structure. I recall an eleven-year-old girl whose father had played Sledge Hammer all her life. A profound depression of the mother led to psychotherapy, and in time she acquired strength and confidence enough to dissolve the marriage. The girl experienced the dissolution of the marriage and her release from Sledge Hammer with frank relief, and in her mother's later remarriage she found a better father than the one she lost; he used no maneuvers and stratagems with her but gave her the love and esteem she sorely needed.

The effect of Tandem Paternity on a child's personality development depends much on the age at which the child has a change of fathers. When the change of fathers occurs during the child's infancy or early childhood, the second father may be the only father with whom the child has much contact, and since "Father is as Father does," the child feels little effect from Tandem Paternity. Much also depends on how much contact the child has with his true father, and on the true father's relationship with the child's mother and her second husband. The fathers may be friendly to each other, or bitterly competitive with each other, or utterly indifferent to one another, and the children may benefit from the situation, or exploit it, or be lost in it, depending on circumstances. The fathers may battle over the care and responsibility of the children, or each one may try to shove the children off on the other whenever possible. When it is time to take a boy fishing, to pay for summer camp, or to chaperon a fourteen-year-old girl to her first dance, each father may try to avoid the responsibility, or they may bicker over who has the privilege of doing it. The child may end up with two competing fathers, or he may be left without an emotionally effective father. Despite all these confusing possibilities, the situation works out reasonably well in the majority of cases. Sometimes the fathers supplement each other, and between their joint efforts they manage to provide one good composite father figure for the child. The true father may function well as a weekend father who would be bored and irritable with the children if he had them all week, and the second father may function well with the children during the week so long as he knows he will be free of them on weekends.

However, Tandem Paternity has its hazards, even when the second father offers a good relationship to the child. These hazards are greatest during adolescence when a certain amount of rebellion and turmoil occurs in even the best-regulated homes. During adolescence the child gradually moves toward more social and emotional independence; he slowly assumes more privileges as the parents gradually relinquish increasing liberty to him, and there frequently are differences of opinion between the child and his parents about just how many privileges the adolescent should have at any particular point. Sometimes the teenager may use the maneuver of "If my true father were here, he'd understand and he'd let me do all the things the other kids are doing." In some instances the true father may exploit the situation to spite his former wife and her second husband; he may commiserate with the child's complaints and approve his rebellious acts and exorbitant demands. The true father can do this with impunity since he sees the adolescent only occasionally and does not have the day-to-day responsibilities of dealing with him. The true father may get unconscious, or even conscious, pleasure out of throwing such bombshells into the home of his former wife and her second husband. In this nasty maneuver the father satisfies his spite by sacrificing the emotional well-being of his child. The maneuver is all the more vicious when the father's theme is: "I'm the only one who understands you; your mother doesn't care and her husband doesn't like you."

When a child has difficulties with his mother and her second husband and has little contact with his true father, he sometimes idealizes the true father *in absentia*. He sometimes envisions the true father as the ideal parent who would solve all problems if he were only here. This may occur even when the true father is rejecting and uninterested in the child. I recall a seventeen-year-old boy in a mild adolescent rebellion who left home and went to a distant city to see his true father, of whom he had seen little during his life and whom he had idealized. He went to his true father's business office and sent in word that he had arrived. The father received him pleasantly, shook hands with him and asked him how he was. After a short while he explained to his son how busy he was, said he could only spend a few more minutes with him and apprehensively asked him if he needed money. The boy returned home more tolerant of his mother and her second husband, who at least were trying to function as parents.

A few women carry out a long hard stratagem of Tandem Paternity and manage to go through three or four marriages in the first two decades of their children's lives. This offers a wide variety of possible maneuvers, stratagems and outright confusion. In Tandem Paternity, a child may survive a doubleheader in good condition. Beyond that, a certain amount of chaos usually sets in.

4

Maneuvers and Stratagems
of Children and Adolescents

In Chapters 2 and 3 we discussed some of the maneuvers and stratagems which parents use with their children, and in this present chapter we shall consider a few of the maneuvers and stratagems children and adolescents sometimes carry out with their parents.

The exploration of childhood has been one of the major accomplishments of twentieth-century psychiatry. Of course, observant persons in previous centuries knew that childhood was not an innocent, blissful blur. They knew that children may have emotional turmoil, misery and cunning and that the personality of the adult is molded gradually by the experiences of the child. However, the scientific study of the emotional life of children is the product of the current century, and public education has diffused this knowledge widely. In a sense, twentieth-century psychiatry "discovered" children.

In Chapters 2 and 3 we traced briefly the basic emotional needs of children. These needs may be summarized as *love, limitations,* and, as he grows older, the *liberty* gradually to become more self-sufficient and independent. A child needs the devoted love of his parents to help him develop a warm, comfortable capacity for interpersonal relationships both in the home and in the broad social world which lies outside it. When the child experiences rejection, hostility and depreciation from his parents, he may develop personality problems and defective capacities for interpersonal living.

A child also needs reasonable limitations set on his behavior and occasional discipline to back up the limitations, in order to develop the capacity to conform to the many restrictions society requires for a good interpersonal adjustment. When he is young, the child's parents put limitations on his behavior; as he grows older, he must internalize those limitations and impose them on himself. Children who have few limitations put on their behavior may have difficulty developing the self-imposed controls which they will need to adjust successfully in adolescence and adulthood. A small boy does not ride his tricycle in the street because his parents put limits on where he may ride; an adult does not speed recklessly on deserted streets at night because he has internalized the limitations and principles of his parents and imposes them on himself.

As the child grows through the years of later childhood and adolescence, his parents must allow him gradually to develop the liberty he will need to function well as an adult. The parents should be neither too possessive nor too permissive. Step by step, and adjusted to what he can handle comfortably at each level, the child gets more privileges. A child can be crippled by parents who cling possessively to him and do not allow him to develop mature independence, or he may flounder badly if his parents shove him out on his own too early without guidance and reasonable controls. Deciding just how much independence an adolescent should have at any age is always a fertile subject for debate between the adolescent, who is straining for more privileges, and his parents, who wonder if he is ready for them.

Throughout childhood and adolescence the intelligence of a child is basically the same as it will be during adulthood. A child's knowledge, skills and judgment increase as he grows older, but his basic intelligence and his capacity for cunning are the same in childhood and adolescence. Hence, a child may show much shrewdness in any maneuvers and stratagems he carries out, and his stratagems may fall at any point in a spectrum which runs from harmlessness to brutality.

During adolescence an individual changes more than during any other period in his subsequent life. At the beginning of adolescence he is emotionally, socially and economically dependent on his parents and their home, but by the end of adolescence he has achieved much emotional, social and economic independence or is in the process of doing so. In addition, the adolescent must adjust to his burgeoning sexuality and develop socially acceptable ways of channeling it. In a sense, adolescence is a test of how stable the previous personality development of the child has been and of the soundness of his relationship with his parents. However, even in the healthiest homes there usually is a certain amount of turmoil as the teenager goes through the dilemmas of adolescence.

We shall now consider a few of the maneuvers and stratagems which children and adolescents sometimes carry out.

Temper Tantrum

Temper Tantrum is one of the most common maneuvers executed by children and adolescents. It usually begins in early childhood, and if the child finds it successful he may carry it into later childhood. In modified forms it may extend into adolescence. Most children make at least a few experiments with this maneuver, and those who find that it works may adopt it as a regular means of manipulating and dominating their parents. It is essentially a put-off maneuver, but it may have corrupt come-on features since it sometimes binds the parents and the child together in an unhealthy relationship.

In Temper Tantrum the child throws himself on the floor, screams loudly, becomes red in the face and bangs his fists and feet on the floor. This may continue from a few minutes to an hour or more. Temper Tantrum usually occurs when the child cannot have his way about something. The wary parent handles Temper Tantrum simply by refusing to become involved in the maneuver. The parent may blithely ignore the child fuming on the floor, or he may dump him in bed and shut the door. For more persistent Temper Tantrums he may use a hairbrush or a belt on the buttocks; this part of the body is well insulated with fat, connective tissue, and thick muscular layers, and hence it is admirably adapted for character-building purposes since swatting cannot inflict any serious physical damage. Ignored, dumped or swatted, the child soon learns that no one will play Temper Tantrum with him and he gives it up.

However, some parents accept the bait and fall right into the maneuver. They plead, coax, threaten or bribe the child to stop; he screams and thrashes harder while the parents become haggard and desperate. In the end, they are so perplexed, frightened or bullied by Temper Tantrum that they give in to the child and do what he wants. The first skirmish is over, and the child has won. However, unless the parents change their tactics, the outcome of the campaign is already decided. The child who carries out good Temper Tantrum maneuvers learns to time his moves skillfully. Some of his favorite times for throwing Temper Tantrums are while waiting with his mother in checkout lines at supermarkets, or just after Daddy comes home from work, or just before company is due to arrive for dinner, or when Mother is hurrying to get dressed to go out. Fortunately, most parents today learn enough about Temper Tantrums from friends, pediatricians and child-rearing booklets to know what to do about this maneuver. However, anxious, confused or gullible parents may still be stampeded by Temper Tantrum, and the grim battle is on.

I recall a fourteen-year-old girl whose parents adhered to the intriguing theory that the only need of a child is "understanding" and that if enough "understanding" is produced in the home, the child blossoms into some type of emotional and intellectual prodigy. They rejected such concepts as limitations and discipline as remains of the prepsychiatric dark ages and proudly viewed *their* home as enlightened and progressive. When the child at the age of three began to throw Temper Tantrums they met the problem by going to the library to get more books on how to "understand" the child better. They also were inveterate attenders of lectures on how to understand children, although they accepted only those points of view which agreed with their own. They explained to skeptical friends and relatives that *their* child was learning to "express herself." Of course, sometimes her "self-expression" could be heard all over the supermarket when her mother demurred on buying some cookies or candy she wanted. Temper Tantrum became the dominant maneuver of their home, and she grew into a demanding, self-centered person with little capacity for tolerating frustration of even her most minor wishes.

Like most Temper Tantrum strategists, her tactics changed somewhat in her later childhood; during her rages she shouted, threw things about her room and threatened to run away. She had chronic conflicts with teachers at school whom she did not obey since she had never learned to obey anyone else. However, she slid through grade school and into high school without any serious school difficulties.

Meanwhile, the parents ransacked the public library for more books on child psychology, since it was clear even to them that she was not getting enough "understanding." Unfortunately, enough new, badly written books on child rearing were published each year to keep them continually supplied with reading material. So she arrived into adolescence, a demanding, self-centered, uncontrolled girl; no one around her had put effective limits on her behavior, and so she had not learned to impose them on herself. However, beneath her façade of arrogant willfulness she was frightened and unsure of herself, for she dimly realized that neither she nor anyone else could put the socially necessary restrictions on her.

At fourteen she refused to attend school, slept until noon, screamed at her parents if they disagreed with her and occasionally threw the breakfast eggs at her mother if she felt they were not correctly cooked. She refused psychiatric consultation when her parents suggested it, and told them, "If you're so sold on psychiatrists, go to one yourselves." This was the only good advice she ever gave her parents, but it arrived ten years too late.

I recall a twenty-four-year-old man who had carried out Temper Tantrum maneuvers all his life. His self-centered, hypochondriacal mother dismissed his behavior problems by observing that he was just like his grandfather and that the grandfather had made a great deal of money in the construction business. His father indulged the boy and admitted that he had "a bit of the old Nick in him," but expressed confidence that he would outgrow it in time. At twenty the boy dropped out of college, married a passive girl, and had two children by her during the next five years. He was unable to hold a job because he quarreled with his superiors at work and became furious if they disagreed with him. He screamed at his children and bullied his wife. On one occasion he took off his belt and flailed his wife with it because dinner was late. His wife was too passive and frightened to get a divorce, and after five years of unhappy marriage she became very depressed and made a serious suicidal attempt with sleeping pills. At this point her family intervened and insisted on long-term psychiatric attention to help her and her disturbed marriage. During the next two years she had much psychotherapy. Her husband made two brief attempts to engage in psychotherapy but did not persist in either one. In time the wife sought a divorce and freed herself from the Temper Tantrum gamut which her husband continued to carry out. After the divorce the husband began to drink heavily to control the anguish and fury which smoldered within him as he gradually perceived that the world would not play Temper Tantrum with him the way his parents had.

Usually, the end result of Temper Tantrum is much less grim

68

than in the two examples cited above. However, a long hard use of Temper Tantrum throughout childhood often produces a demanding, easily angered person who has chronic minor conflicts at home, at work and in his social relationships. If the world furnishes him a comfortable life in which most of his demands are met, the Temper Tantrum strategist may be charming and affable. However, he often responds to the buffets and disappointments of life with fury, despair and depression.

The trouble with Temper Tantrum is that the world won't respond the way the person's parents did, and if Temper Tantrum is the main maneuver the person learned during his childhood and adolescence, he is in for a lot of trouble.

Divide and Rule

Divide and Rule, in which the child plays his parents off against each other, is one of the most devastating put-off stratagems a child can execute, and it may begin in early childhood and continue throughout later childhood and adolescence. Most children make at least a few experiments with this stratagem, but if the child encounters a united front in his parents he soon abandons it. However, the child who discovers that by Divide and Rule he can manipulate his parents and dominate his home soon begins to work this stratagem in earnest. In doing so, he is setting the stage for much misery for his parents and some unhealthy personality developments in himself.

Minor, occasional maneuvers of Divide and Rule are common. For example, when chastised by his mother, the child runs to his father with the "that woman is persecuting me again" approach. Of course, the child puts it in simpler, more subtle words by saying, "I didn't do anything; why is Mother so mad at me all the time?" or "It wasn't my fault, so why is she taking it out on me?" If father falls into the trap he says something like "Lay off the kid, Margie; don't take it out on him just because you're upset," or "You always nag these kids unbearably when it's this time of the month for you." A quarrel ensues between the parents while the child cowers triumphantly behind the father's chair or quietly sneaks off to do what he wanted to do in the first place.

The cunning with which some children carry out Divide and Rule may equal that of the Hapsburgs, to whom the phrase "Divide and Rule" was applied in describing their Machiavellian methods of controlling the many small national groups which composed the Austro-Hungarian Empire. Anyone who has watched a shrewd seven-year-old child carry off a skillful stratagem of Divide and Rule and thus contribute to bringing his parents to the brink of divorce will abandon forever his illusions about what used to be called the Age of Innocence. A good Divide and Rule strategist has an uncanny ability to diagnose and exploit whatever weaknesses exist in his parents' marriage. For example, a small girl may grasp intuitively that her mother is somewhat competitive with men and on the defensive about any attempts of men to act superior toward her. As early as the age of four this girl may begin to exploit the theme "Why does Daddy let my little brother do lots of things he won't let me do? Is it fair, Mommy?" With bland innocence in her tearful eyes, this artful disciple of Machiavelli has discovered the one vulnerable point in her parents' marriage, and she sharpens her stilettos to insert and twist.

In a similar way, a small boy may play his father off against his mother. He accompanies each mild spanking by his mother with screaming loud enough to be elicited by the most ingenious tortures of the Spanish Inquisition. He is careful to shriek loud enough so that his father, who is replacing a fuse in the basement, can hear clearly the anguish of his "mistreated child" who is receiving a few mild swats in a second-floor bedroom behind a closed door. Following this punishment, the child carefully sniffles and rubs his eyes (rubbing makes them red and increases the sorrowful appearance) all through dinner while the father makes soothing remarks to him and glares at the mother. When the child plays the mother off against the father, the mother's theme is: "When you come home upset from the office, don't take it out on poor Karen," or "Teddy isn't to blame just because you had a bad month in sales; don't take out your failures on him." Though the child may begin the stratagem by throwing a little kindling on the small sparks of his parents' discord, the parents soon join in and throw buckets of gasoline onto the blaze.

Children who execute Divide and Rule often involve their brothers and sisters in the stratagem. A skillful strategist can divide the family into two teams, almost as if he were saying, "Now, we'll put Cathy on Daddy's team, and Mother and I will be on the other team. All right, let's all go at it." In some instances, the Divide and Rule strategist senses the favoritism of one parent for another child and the partiality of the other parent toward the strategist himself. A Divide and Rule expert is quick to take advantage of such a situation; the possibilities for domestic misery are legion, and it's a fast, easy stratagem to work. The strategist continually provokes his brother or sister into fights, then runs screaming to the parent who favors him and reports, "Mike is picking on me again and Daddy won't stop him." Mother indignantly proclaims, "I'll straighten this out." She takes off her apron and strides into the family room to "straighten out" Father and the persecuting child, who may be from one to several years younger than the child she is defending. Father is ready to do battle for his favorite, and a first-rate fight ensues. Divide and Rule experts also are adept at making the most of minor scratches and bruises they receive from other children in the family. "Look what Harry did to me"—"I'll put a bandage on it, darling, and then take care of Harry," is a good opener for an evening of misery in a home where Divide and Rule is being skillfully carried out.

Sometimes a child operates Divide and Rule by pitting a grandparent and a parent against each other. In a commonly encountered situation, the child plays his mother off against his paternal grandmother; the child cunningly is taking advantage of the fact that his paternal grandmother is his mother's mother-in-law. The diabolical possibilities of this combination are obvious. Some of Grandmother's favorite leitmotivs are: "I raised three children and I know more things about raising them than some of these modern mothers [referring, of course, to her daughter-in-law, the child's mother] who spend all their time in beauty shops and going to cocktail parties," and "If I did such a bad job and know so little about raising children, why did that girl [the child's mother] pick out my son to marry?" and "I don't see why Marty [her son] lets Evelyn [her daughter-in-law] mistreat poor little Billy [the six-year-old Divide and Rule expert] so much." Sometimes Grandmother lives in the same home with her son, his wife and the grandchild; then Divide and Rule reaches its most refined state.

I recall a nine-year-old girl who had been carrying out a successful Divide and Rule operation with her parents since she was three. Her father was a meticulous, somewhat officious man whom she had seduced into the role of her advocate and defender against the mother. Her mother was an effusive, affectionate woman who, however, had a temper which could flash out suddenly when she was properly stimulated. The child was an expert at stimulating her mother's fury and then manipulating her father's pious indignation in defending her against the mother's rage. The parents' marriage had deteriorated into miserable chaos, largely owing to the child's brilliant use of Divide and Rule. The father wanted to divorce the mother, but feared she might get major custody of the child in the divorce settlement, and he could not "deliver the poor child into the hands of that woman." I undertook to do family counseling with this family. During my second interview with the father, the mother arrived in the waiting room of my office with the child and a suitcase full of the child's clothing. She summoned the father and me to the waiting room and announced she was through with all of us, was leaving the girl with the father and was taking the two younger children back to live in her mother's home in Pennsylvania. I was able to calm her down and sent all of them home. This situation had deteriorated so badly that we arranged to send our little Divide and Rule expert to a therapeutically run school in California for a year while I did family counseling with the parents. When the girl returned to live at home, she found that her parents would no longer play Divide and Rule with her. With continued counseling of the mother and father for another year, the situation turned out well. Years later I met her parents socially, and they told me that our little Divide and Rule strategist had matured into an intelligent, sophisticated young lady who was doing well in graduate school and wanted to enter the diplomatic service. I observed that if she were appointed ambassador to the Soviet Union she could probably widen the schism between that country and China.

Immovable Object

The child or adolescent who carries out Immovable Object baits and infuriates his parents by failing to do most of the things they expect of him. He moves with foot-dragging slowness and bumbling inefficiency while his parents rage and fume impotently at him. He especially resists them in areas in which they cannot easily punish him, as, for example, in poor learning achievement and apparent stupidity in school. By passive resistance he skewers his parents on a spit over a hot fire and slowly turns. Immovable Object is fueled by strong put-off feelings in the child.

In Immovable Object the child unconsciously sacrifices his achievements and social development; at this cost he retaliates his parents for the rejection, hostility or lovelessness he has experienced from them. His smoldering hostility toward his parents finds unhealthy release in his foot-dragging inability to fulfill their expectations and demands. This stratagem may begin in early childhood

73

and continue throughout adolescence into early adulthood. Immovable Object is played for high stakes, and both the child and his parents often pay severe penalties. None of the players has a conscious awareness of the emotional forces which drive him on in the grim, stubborn stratagem in which he is engaged.

I recall a sixteen-year-old boy who was brought to me because of persistent failure in school and poor social adjustment. His parents complained that he "never seemed to do anything right." He was a tall, awkward boy who stared blankly at me and answered my questions in brief, evasive sentences. He shambled slowly in and out of the office and did not show pleasure, distaste, anger or anxiousness about any topic we discussed. He approached everything with a wooden facial expression and physical immobility. Each year he either failed in high school or managed to scrape by with the lowest possible passing grades, yet psychological testing showed superior intelligence. When his parents asked him to do some task in the house, he was so slow or broke so many things that they rarely asked him to do it again. Although his father continually fumed at him about his table manners, the boy continued to spill his food and to eat noisily with his mouth open.

His father was a businessman who found his son's lack of achievement infuriating. While his friends discussed the athletic and scholastic achievements of their sons he was reduced to the dull hope that his awkward son would be able to graduate from high school. The sharpest stabs to the father came when his friends discussed the colleges their sons hoped to enter and asked what his son was planning to do. By systematically doing nothing at all, this boy had devised the most exquisite torture possible for his socially and economically ambitious father.

This boy was born six months after his father went overseas in World War II. He was the firstborn child, and his parents had not wanted a child so soon; they had planned not to begin their family until a few years after the father returned from the Army. The boy's birth prevented the mother from working while the father was in military service, and they had planned to save the money the mother made to help the father begin a small electrical contracting business when he came home. When the boy was eighteen months old the father came home from military service. He openly resented sharing his wife with the child who took up much of her time. He complained about the annoyances of having a baby in the house during what he called his "second honeymoon" on returning from service, and he labeled him a "difficult kid."

The mother was affectionate toward the child, but the father was rejecting, irritable and critical toward the boy throughout his childhood and adolescence. As the months and years went by, the father's persistent resentment of his son began to produce the inadequacies of which he accused him. The mother was a passive person who rarely resisted her husband on any issue, and she did not interfere with his browbeating and belittling of the boy. She hesitated to show her underlying fondness for the boy and thus incur the irritability of her husband, who told her to "stop mollycoddling that boy and making excuses for all the things he does." The faults of the father toward this boy were the faults of commission, and the faults of the mother were those of omission.

From the age of two onward, this boy began his stratagem of Immovable Object. He never rebelled or refused to do what he was told, but the repressed hostility within him required some outlet. This hostility began to come out in a foot-dragging inability to do whatever his father commanded or his mother implored. Toilet training was an endless mess, both literally and figuratively, and even at the age of four he occasionally soiled himself. Getting ready to go to bed was a time-consuming ritual during which his father fumed loudly and his mother pleaded in whispers. Discipline accomplished nothing, since in the absence of love and respect for a child, punishment often creates as many problems as it solves.

When the boy entered school Immovable Object took an ominous turn, for he intuitively had grasped that his socially ambitious father very much wanted him to do well in school. He stared

75

blankly at the teachers and did not learn. Special tutoring, promises of rewards for good grades and threats of punishment for failures only froze him more solidly in poor school achievement. Unconsciously he had found his father's tenderest point, and he continually probed it with jagged fishhooks. He also was poor in athletics during his school years and conspicuously awkward in his social relationships. His father cringed each time he had to introduce his silent, gangling son to friends or business acquaintances who came to their home. On such occasions the boy came forward with a weak handshake, stood dumbly staring at the visitors, and had nothing to say as they vainly tried to engage him in small talk.

Thus, Immovable Object ground on through the boy's later childhood and adolescence. His distraught father alternated between "I always said the boy was a total loss" and "Maybe he'll outgrow it in time." When the boy was sixteen the family doctor suggested psychiatric consultation, and the father said he was willing to do anything that might help. The boy's problems at this time were no worse than they had always been. However, when he was young his difficulties could be hidden from the father's friends, but as he approached manhood his problems were glaring. Both the boy and his father were caught in the vicious circle which Immovable Object often creates; the more the father raged, the more the boy balked.

Psychotherapy with this family was difficult and only partially successful. Attempts to involve the father in counseling to help him change his attitudes toward the boy were fruitless. He frankly stated, "Straighten this boy out; my only responsibility is to pay the bills to get the job done." The mother was more approachable in psychotherapy, and in a dim way she had known for many years what the basic problem was. However, she had been too timid and unsure of herself to do anything about it. By working in individual psychotherapy sessions with both the mother and the boy, we were able to diminish the intensity of Immovable Object. The boy gained some insight into the hostility he was expressing in his lack of achievement, and he also responded slowly to the earnest interest and respect for him that the psychiatrist's activities implied. He found a good father figure in the psychiatrist, and he cautiously explored in his relationship with the psychiatrist the possibility that a father-son relationship could be something more than a stubborn exchange of hostility and negativism.

In time, this boy graduated from high school and entered a small liberal arts college, but he rejected his father's demands that he should plan his education to prepare himself to enter the father's electrical contracting business. He stuck to his intention to go into commercial art, for in late adolescence he had begun to show talent in this field. The father blamed his son's psychiatrist for the boy's decision and bitterly complained that he had "lost his son" because the boy would not join him in business. Though the father actually had lost his son during the boy's childhood, he realized it only when the boy reached manhood and a wide gulf lay between them. The stratagem of Immovable Object was over. The participants retired from the field and went their separate ways.

Different Breed of Cat

In the stratagem of Different Breed of Cat, which is executed mainly by adolescents, the teenager seeks to establish his independence and individuality by developing customs, standards and behavior which are strikingly different from those of his parents; it is a classic kind of put-off stratagem. To a certain extent, a majority of adolescents carry out mild stratagems of Different Breed of Cat. The boys let their hair grow long and the girls wear their skirts very short. Sons of rock-ribbed political conservatives become blatant liberals, and the children of liberals vaunt conservative slogans. Adolescents carry out mild varieties of Different Breed of

77

Cat in clothing, grooming, speech idioms and the ways they entertain themselves.

A mild degree of Different Breed of Cat may be considered within normal limits. It is a fumbling way in which the teenager gradually works through the process of ceasing to be a child and becoming an independent adult. Although in Different Breed of Cat the adolescent may caricature the process of becoming independent, the stratagem often is harmless and may even serve some useful purposes. For example, it may help an insecure, shy adolescent break loose from the parental home and become more self-confident.

The harmlessness or malignity of Different Breed of Cat often depends on the wisdom of the parents involved in it. If the parents precipitate major crises in Different Breed of Cat, they may push the teenager into grotesque rebellion which exceeds the normal limits of adolescence. Other parents may squelch the first faint stirrings of individuality in a timid, insecure adolescent whom they thus cram back into a docile, homebound role. Sometimes it is better to tolerate Different Breed of Cat as a healthy adventure. Many parents must steer a moderate course, tolerating the socially acceptable aspects of Different Breed of Cat and attempting to modify its unacceptable extremes. To decide the precise point at which Different Breed of Cat becomes unacceptable and unhealthy often taxes the judgment of parents, and the adolescent and his parents frequently disagree. Being a parent probably is the most difficult job in the world, and no one is an expert at it. The most important job any generation faces is to rear the next generation which will succeed it; people are the most crucial product a society produces.

However, the stratagem of Different Breed of Cat becomes serious when it results in a full-scale rebellion of the adolescent against the standards and customs of his parents. When carried to extremes, Different Breed of Cat leads businessmen's sons to rob filling stations and ministers' daughters to become sexually promiscuous. I recall a seventeen-year-old boy who carried out a tragic stratagem of Different Breed of Cat. His father was a politically ambitious attorney who had paid little attention to the boy during the boy's formative years, and the boy's mother had turned him over to an ever-shifting stream of maids and babysitters while she accompanied her husband on a treadmill of social activities. The boy grew into adolescence with much unconscious resentment against his parents who had so little time for him and so much time for everyone else. When his parents had prolonged contact with him, their habitual indifference to the boy turned to irritable impatience. In his early adolescence the boy began his operation of Different Breed of Cat as he unconsciously sought a role completely different from that of his parents. All his life they had rejected him, and now it was his turn to reject them. When he was fourteen he drove the family car and was arrested for speeding and driving without a license. The father went down to the police station, and because of his influence in the community, the matter was dropped. However, the boy had stumbled on a way to be a Different Breed of Cat and at the same time to revenge himself on his father and mother by humiliating them socially. The stratagem began in deadly earnest.

By the age of sixteen the boy was a hanger-on at filling stations and drugstores where high-school dropouts and aspirant juvenile delinquents congregated. He dressed in tight clothing which seemed designed to cover the greatest possible area of his body with the least square feet of cloth. He sported a black leather jacket with a lascivious dragon painted on the back, and he hid his motorcycle in the garage of a friend. He routinely failed his subjects in school, managing only to pass driver's education, and he became expert in baiting the teachers. He could make "Yes, sir" and "No, ma'am" sound like insults as they slithered off the end of his tongue. His parents' social and political influence prevented his expulsion from school but could not secure him passing grades. His parents sent him away to a private boys' school in Arizona, but he left after five weeks and hitchhiked home. When he was seventeen he was arrested three times for shoplifting, but his father each time arranged to have the charges dropped. His chaotic rebellion against everything his parents represented became more ominous, while his anguished parents sought desperately for measures to stop his social deterioration. His revenge on his parents for their long neglect of him was delicious, although he could not put his delight consciously into words as he saw them squirm helplessly while he dragged them through social disgrace and unsavory notoriety. However, he was destroying himself in the process.

At eighteen he was arrested after breaking into a filling station late at night and stealing thirty dollars. His troubles now were too severe to escape punishment, but his father's intervention resulted in securing a mild punishment of four months' confinement in a county correctional home located in their city. He repeatedly ran away from this correctional home, an offense which usually resulted in transfer to a large prisonlike reformatory in the center of the state. However, the officials hesitated to take such a step because of the father's influence, and the boy taunted the officials that they "couldn't touch" him because of his influential family. Six weeks after entering the correctional home he ran away, stole a car and was caught by the state highway police. After this he was given a two-year sentence to the maximum-security reform institution in the center of the state. He was now a completely Different Breed of Cat. In some kinds of maneuvers and stratagems, both sides lose disastrously.

However, the end result of Different Breed of Cat usually is less serious; the stratagem may even be amusing to the uninvolved spectator although the participants usually go through a fair amount of misery. In fact, most stratagems of Different Breed of Cat are self-limiting; the adolescent establishes his triumphant individuality, he no longer needs the stratagem, and he drops it. I recall a seventeen-year-old girl who flourished a long cigarette holder before her bewildered parents as she talked of "the sexual revolution," "the stodginess of virginity," and the advisability of "frequent trial marriages" beginning in midadolescence. She often brought these topics up before her parents' friends, and remonstrances from her parents evoked a smile of pity from her as she patronizingly chided them for their "hopelessly outdated ideas and customs." After several years of tormenting her parents and flaunting her individuality, she gave up this masquerade and settled down to a sedate suburban life. Her parents are waiting with undisguised vengeful anticipation for the day when this girl's children begin their own adolescent stratagems of Different Breed of Cat.

Body Talk

In the stratagems we have discussed so far, the main interplay between people has involved words and actions, what people said and did to each other. However, reactions to interpersonal problems are not always expressed in words and actions between people; sometimes they are manifested in body reactions which express defiance, or yearnings for affection, or sadness, or fury, or sexual passion. The person does nothing and says nothing toward the other person. Instead, his body talks.

Everyone is familiar with Body Talk in some way or other. The anxious salesman who cannot talk back to customers or defy his sales manager instead may soothe his twisting stomach with antacid pills and stomach relaxants. The worried student may express his fear of impending examinations by diarrhea; some psychiatrists have advanced the fanciful speculation that he symbolically is expressing what he thinks of the world by defecating on it. I once had a patient who broke out in hives every time she saw her boyfriend, even if he was a block away. The varieties of Body Talk are almost as numerous as the many functions of the body's major organ systems. People cramp, defecate, belch, itch, bleed, blush, collapse, pant, gasp for air, and ache in any limb or appendage in

81

the many forms of Body Talk that take the place of words, awareness of feelings and actions. Properly speaking, Body Talk is not a stratagem. It is a special type of body response which may be grafted onto any kind of maneuver or stratagem. Body Talk may occur at any age from infancy to old age, but we shall consider only Body Talk in children.

A dramatic form of Body Talk in children is fecal soiling. A clear, if less elegant, term is defecation in the pants; the child dribbles feces into his underwear several times each day. The child who has fecal soiling may never have been successfully toilet-trained, or he may return to soiling after he has been toilet-trained for several years. We here are discussing children of normal intelligence who are physically well. In these children, fecal soiling several times a day is a form of Body Talk which expresses smoldering, pent-up feelings which the child cannot express in words and actions. The strong odor which chronically radiates from these children creates havoc in the parent-child relationships and causes marked problems at school and in other social situations. In 1926 an industrious German physician gave this problem the name of encopresis, which added some medical dignity to the condition but shed no light on it.

The first physician to describe this form of Body Talk in children was an American, Dr. G. B. Fowler, who reported a case of it in a medical journal in 1882. His patient was a seven-year-old boy who had been crammed with knowledge by his ambitious parents. He astonished his parents' friends and relatives with the amounts of information he could spout forth on command. "Under such conditions," Dr. Fowler wrote, "it is not to be wondered that something gave way and, fortunately for the brain, it was the anal sphincter."

I recall a five-year-old boy who was seldom without a small puddle of feces in his underwear despite his mother's harried efforts to change his clothing and wash him off several times each day. The boy's continuous distinctive odor caused consternation in his mother, ridicule in the neighborhood and repeated conferences between the mother and the kindergarten teacher. Sunday School had been abandoned because the child's malodor caused continual gibing comments from other children which were not harmonious with the Sunday School atmosphere.

The boy's mother was an unceasing striver for cleanliness and order. She spent her days endlessly cleaning and arranging the house. She could not tolerate dirty ashtrays, unwashed dishes or closet doors ajar. Her husband sighed resignedly and meekly complained that life in their home was like living in an immaculate museum. The crucial battle between this obsessively clean mother and her normally disorderly child came in the toilet-training period. Mother coaxed, fussed and scolded the child too early and too fast into toilet training. He was a passive, timid boy who could not fight back with howls and actions, so he rebelled with his body. In fecal soiling he unconsciously found a way to jab his mother in her most vulnerable spot. Toilet training became a stubbornly fought battle between them, and the boy's pent-up rage against his controlling mother erupted in defiant defecation.

The child's continual foul odor finally forced his mother reluctantly to bring him for psychiatric help. I saw both the boy and his mother in separate counseling sessions for five months. Counseling with the mother dealt with how her unhealthy needs for cleanliness and control of her child were corrupting her relationship with him and contributing to his soiling. The mother begrudgingly accepted some of my suggestions and altered some aspects of her behavior toward the child. However, her ill-concealed resentment toward me glimmered through in such comments as "Well, why isn't your office as messy as you would like my home to be?" or "Does your wife leave your house all cluttered up all the time?" I avoided these uncomfortable inquiries by the old psychiatric dodge of answering a question with a question. However, she was able to change enough to give the boy a home atmosphere in which he could solve his problem.

My sessions with the boy were spent in helping him release some of the hostility which smoldered in him toward his mother. In play therapy sessions with him we made buildings of blocks and then savagely wrecked them by racing toy cars into them. While engaged in such hostile play, we talked about how it was better to get anger out of your system by blowing off a little steam than by dirtying your pants all the time. We also did finger painting. As we sloshed the messy paints on paper we talked about how it was better to be comfortable with a little dirt and sloppiness than to be as meticulously neat as his mother was. In time the boy became more comfortable with his anger and occasionally began to defy his mother. He ceased to be a passive, malodorous child and became a normally assertive, occasionally cantankerous, nonodorous boy. Although mother was pleased that the soiling stopped, she was dismayed that her child was less docile. She observed that he had been a much nicer little boy before he had "all this psychiatry business."

Many other kinds of Body Talk occur in children, and often they can lose these dysfunctions if they learn to convert their Body Talk into words and actions with people. I recall a passive seven-year-old boy with a stomach ulcer who never expressed assertiveness or anger and let everyone bully him. Treatment of this boy consisted of weekly counseling sessions with him and his mother separately to help the boy become more assertive. He became able to stick up for himself in the neighborhood and to talk back occasionally to his parents, and in time his ulcer healed.

In one of our final sessions the mother reported that her son was doing well but that he had had a little trouble at school. On the playground he had bloodied the nose of a bully who had long tormented him. The principal called him to his office and asked the boy why he had done this. Our seven-year-old patient replied, "Because my psychiatrist told me to." The principal did nothing because he knew the boy had long been tormented by the bully, but he called the mother to find out what was going on. When the mother explained, the principal said, "Well, I've heard a lot of reasons for fighting on the playground, but that's the first time I ever heard that one." One rarely encounters a case which so clearly demonstrates the conversion of Body Talk into interpersonal action.

5

Marital Maneuvers and Stratagems

Marriage is the most intimate relationship which occurs between two adults. It is sanctioned by law, ushered in by a religious ceremony, and in many instances it lasts until death. It changes a woman's name and changes how the couple look at society and how society looks at them. No other interpersonal relationship demands so much of the people who enter into it. They must coordinate their wishes, vanities, dislikes, plans and personality quirks. They must jointly pay bills, rear children, have sex, furnish houses, get along with each other's relatives and eat the same kinds of food. When you consider that the two persons have different personalities, come from different family backgrounds and usually have known each other for only a small part of their lives, the possibilities for trouble are great. Marriage surpasses all other adult relationships in the possible combinations of maneuvers and stratagems, and of put-offs and come-ons. If the couple achieve happiness in this relationship they have something valuable; if not, they may end up with a two-way, reverberating, self-propelled torture circuit which is the nearest thing to perpetual motion yet devised by the ingenuity of man.

We shall consider a few of the maneuvers and stratagems of marriage. Let them be a warning to the unwary and a guide to the wise.

The Maneuvers and Stratagems of Courtship

A wide variety of maneuvers and stratagems and put-offs and come-ons may occur during courtship. Such diverse put-off and come-on forces as passion, convenience, escape from boredom, money, pity, hostile competition, reasonable hopes, doomed expectations, fear, guilt, desperation, lust and affection may enter into these maneuvers and stratagems. We shall describe briefly a few of the common maneuvers and stratagems of courtship.

Love Will Come Later

This stratagem occurs between a girl and her mother. Marvin has proposed to Deborah, and Deborah is in doubt, severe doubt. Marvin is a nice boy, comes from a "good family," has a good income, belongs to the right country club, knows which fork to use for salads, and is in all other ways an excellent catch. The one nagging problem is that Deborah does not love him; in fact, she's not sure she even likes him very much. He has fat hands and a wide, pasty face, and his conversation is dull. He's been an acceptable escort for nine months of dating since he always takes Deborah to fashionable places and good parties where she can talk to lots of fun people. Marvin is a nice fellow, but Deborah cringes at the prospect of his escorting her to bed on her honeymoon. She feels like shrinking when he touches her. However, she can't explain these things to her mother, and she's not sure she can explain them to herself. Deborah cannot think of any concrete reasons why she shouldn't marry Marvin, except that she doesn't love him.

Mother now executes a skillful maneuver. Mother feels sure

86

that she knows what is best better than Deborah, and in the past Mother has always managed to dominate Deborah on crucial decisions. Mother's maneuver centers on the theme "After you're married, dear, and have sex together, you'll get to love him. I know. After all, I didn't love your father when I married him." Only the latter part of this statement may be true; the first part is a deceptive path to marital misery.

Since Deborah has led a sheltered life, dominated by mother, she has not yet got around to having sex with a boy, and so she can't debate the subject on equal ground with Mother. Even if Deborah has had a few experiments with sex she is not in a good position to tell Mother about them and to protest that bedroom calisthenics, in her limited experience, have not produced love. Mother therefore has marshaled an unanswerable argument to propel Deborah to the marriage altar. Mother skillfully has chosen a battleground on which Deborah cannot defend herself well; she has outmaneuvered her. Every discussion of Marvin—and there are many—ends with Deborah's plaintive objection that she doesn't love him, and Mother then annihilates Deborah with the Love Will Come Later stratagem.

If Mother executes her stratagem well, she carries the day. She wins an alliance with Marvin's family and with all the drugstores, jewelry shops or insurance agencies they own. Mother's prestige at the club and the bridge table goes up. Father, a somewhat henpecked man, retreats behind his cigar and "leaves these things to the women." The only one who loses is Deborah. Her honeymoon is drab, and her marriage is tasteless. The final act of Love Will Come Later often is played out years later in doctors' offices or divorce courts.

Salvation Army Lass

The theme of this stratagem of courtship is: "All Fred needs is a good little wife to settle him down. You're just the girl to do the job." This stratagem may be thought up by the girl herself to dispel her doubts, or it may be promulgated by the girl's family, by the boy's family, by meddlesome friends or by other purveyors of disaster. It is an insidious path to marital misery and helps supply the money which sends the children of divorce lawyers to Ivy League colleges.

The boy's defects which the girl is urged to remedy by marrying him may include unemployability, alcoholism, financial irresponsibility, running around with "the wrong kind of women," "nervousness," or incapacitating hypochondriasis. The boy's mother usually is sweet, his father is a solid citizen, and his family is "good." The promulgators of this stratagem urge that he will straighten out after marriage. All he needs is a good little wife to bring out the sound stuff hidden under all his obvious defects. The epigram about "sowing a few wild oats" is lightly tossed around as the girl convinces herself to marry the boy, or others persuade her to do it, and by this signal act to dazzle everybody with his subsequent reformation. She puts on her Salvation Army Lass uniform and wades in to redeem a soul.

However, personality problems are not eradicated by a twenty-minute wedding ceremony. Marriage requires intimate adjustments by two people to each other in a new kind of life; it is more likely to create a few problems than to solve any. Unemployability, irresponsibility, and alcoholism are more likely to be aggravated by marriage than cured by it. However, the girl is so intoxicated by the nobility of her act and the dazzling results she anticipates that she confidently brushes aside the skepticism of friends or the alarm of relatives. The boy may be good-looking, charming and a ready conversationalist; he may have all the glitter and none of the substance of a good husband. In addition, the girl may be in love with him. The boy usually is in love with himself and accepts the girl's adulation as his inherent due.

They have a wonderful courtship, a gay round of prewedding parties, a honeymoon that makes her dreams come true and a blissful return home. Disillusionment comes after the first baby, despair after the second one, and divorce after the third.

The Eternal Boyfriend

The typical man who is engaged in this stratagem is between his early thirties and his late fifties. He has a good job and acceptable table manners. He is a good talker at parties, plays respectable golf, bowls on Thursday nights and is, all in all, a preeminently eligible bachelor. He has a history of nearly being engaged or nearly married three or four times, but somehow it never came off. His friends are chronically introducing him to nice girls who are eager to get married. He is forever dating a new girl and "waiting for the right girl to come along." He is good-looking despite thinning hair at his temples, and a weekly workout at the gym keeps him from getting too flabby. He has been best man more times than he can count on his fingers and is a reliable resource for being godfather to squalling children who grow up to call him "Uncle Bill" and expect Christmas presents from him. He is always on the verge of "getting serious," and everyone is sure that they will see him married to "that cute little Lewis girl before next summer."

However, it's all a stratagem. He is the Eternal Boyfriend. He's scared, and he may or may not know it. For example, he may be scared of getting caught in a bad marriage such as his parents had. Everyone is much affected by the emotional atmosphere of his parents' marriage, and the bliss or misery of that marriage has a marked effect on what the person longs for or dreads in a marriage of his own. In other cases, the Eternal Boyfriend is sexually impotent, as he has discovered with call girls or in a few sexual adventures with girlfriends. At other times, the Eternal Boyfriend is terrified of responsibility, of children, of mothers-in-law, or of all the other paraphernalia of marriage, and he may or may not know it.

His course is predictable. He proceeds from his dashing twenties into his debonair thirties and wends his way through his flirtatious forties into his mature fifties. The single girls who set traps for him when he was in his twenties and thirties are replaced by the divorcées who lay subtler, but equally ineffective, snares for him in his forties and fifties. By the time he arrives in his early forties, many of his friends have seen through his stratagem and no longer expect him ever to marry, but there always are restless divorcées and hopeful unmarried girls who are willing to make one more try. Once in a while a clever girl catches one of these elusive birds, and he often makes a better husband than would be expected. Once he gets pushed into the water he may not find it as cold as he expected, and he may be a better swimmer than he thought. However, marriage licenses are not sold with guarantees.

The Roommate Stratagem

"The three girls I roomed with all got married and I was left alone in the apartment. I really didn't love David, but he was persistent, and so we got married." This is a common stratagem of girls from Chillicothe or Springfield who are working in San Francisco or New York. A better tactic is to scout around for three more roommates in the typing pool at work. Roommates are easier to get rid of than husbands and children.

The Escape Maneuver

"I couldn't stand all the fighting between Mom and her second husband. Larry offered to marry me, and so I got out." This dangerous way to make the marital plunge sometimes works out well, but the risks are high. The girl often is so busy running from her parents' home that she doesn't take a good look at the marriage she's getting into. The solution to the Escape Maneuver is to get a job, move out of the house, and then look for a husband at leisure.

How to Run from the Altar

Scene: Mother's bedroom. Time: two days before the wedding. Characters: Sobbing daughter, flustered mother and perplexed father.

Wrong Kind of Maneuver

DAUGHTER: But, Mother I don't love him. I can't go through with it. I just can't stand it when he kisses me.

MOTHER: Honey, you're just nervous. All girls are nervous before they get married. You'll get over this. Now pull yourself together.

FATHER: We can't call the wedding off now. We've invited all these people, it's been in the newspapers, and what would we do with those three rooms full of wedding presents downstairs?

DAUGHTER: Oh, Lord, I'll go through with it. I hope I'm doing the right thing.

MOTHER: Of course, you are, darling. Everything will be all right.

FATHER: Sure, baby. Hes' a fine young man. Now let's go downstairs. The Franklins are arriving and they'll want to see you.

Right Kind of Maneuver

Same scene. Same time. Same cast.

DAUGHTER: But, Mother, I don't love him. I can't go through with it. I just can't stand it when he kisses me.

MOTHER: Well, honey, think it over until tomorrow morning. If you really don't want to marry him, you can still back out.

FATHER: We want you to be happy, baby doll.

DAUGHTER: But how will I ever face all those people? How will I tell Ed that I don't want to marry him and I can't go through with it?

FATHER (somewhat choked up, fishing for his wallet): Honey, think it over for a couple of hours or until tomorrow morning. Here's the money. Call a taxi early tomorrow and grab an early plane to St. Louis. Your Aunt Fran and Uncle Ben will be glad to put you up for a couple of months. Get a job and come back when it's all blown over.

DAUGHTER: Thanks, Mom. Thanks, Dad. You're wonderful. (Goes into the next room to pack a suitcase.)

MOTHER: My Lord, John, what are we going to do now? What are we going to tell Ed? What are we going to do with all those wedding presents? Look, there are the Franklins coming up the walk with a big package. Oh, Lord!

FATHER: Well, we've seen our little girl through twenty years of little crises and troubles. We can't run out on her now. I think I'll pour myself a double Scotch. The next three or four days are going to be rough.

MOTHER: Pour one for me, too.

Peck Order

If a group of chickens are put together in an enclosed yard, they soon establish a social hierarchy of dominance and submission. Some chickens habitually peck other chickens on their heads; the pecked chickens are submissive to those who peck them, and do not peck back. The chickens who are pecked in turn peck other chickens who are lower than they in this hierarchy. Thus, a social system is formed in the shape of a pyramid, with a few supreme chickens at the top and tiers of lower social levels below them. Biologists call this a peck order.

The same phenomenon may occur in marriage. Many maneuvers and stratagems are executed in the struggle to determine which member of the marital team will be dominant and which one will be submissive. The final result is a marital Peck Order. Peck Order is basically a put-off stratagem. However, when it becomes ingrained and the couple are bound together in it, it may have a come-on influence.

Some people are domineering and others seek strong, decisive people to lean on. In some instances the nature of the marital Peck Order can be foretold before the wedding. "Jean will wear the pants in that family" or "Tom will be boss in that home" may be common knowledge of the friends of an engaged couple. The engaged couple may know it themselves and accept it. A passive, dependent girl may say, "I don't want to be boss. I want Tom to be the man of the house." If Tom is considerate and affectionate as well as dominant, the marriage may satisfy the personality needs of each one. If Tom bullies her and exploits her passivity, the marriage may be a miserable trap for her. A Sledge Hammer stratagem (see Chapter 3) may ensue. In other instances the wife is dominant and the husband accepts her leadership; if she exercises her reign with moderation they may get along well. On the other hand, if she bullies her husband and exploits his dependence, their home may deteriorate into miserable chaos. In the healthiest marriages both husband and wife have flexible capacities for give-and-take, and neither wants to be dominant or submissive; a Peck Order struggle does not occur.

In some marriages the battle to determine the Peck Order goes on for years or decades. Sometimes a stable Peck Order is never established; truces occur in the chronic war, but a final settlement is never reached. The entrenched couple battle on until a divorce court, death or senile disability brings the contest to an end.

When marital partners are evenly matched and each has a strong need to dominate, they use a fascinating battery of weapons against each other. When one of them finds a new weapon, his advanced technology for a while gives him the ascendancy. Then the other marital partner discovers a defense against the new weapon or develops an even better weapon, and the battle seesaws back the other way. Some couples are famous among their acquaintances for the ingenuity of their battles; relatives and friends look on with fascination and horror as the couple mutilate each other from year to year. In some instances one of them finally establishes a Peck Order ascendancy over the other. However, this dominance may last only a few months; then the subdued partner revolts and the struggle begins again. Occasionally they both burn out, or at least reduce the intensity of their Peck Order struggle, and settle down to minor sniping as beleaguered equals.

Peck Order strategists may or may not be unhappy in their struggles. Though some are miserable, others thrive on the fray. Others tire of the struggle in time, call it quits and go their separate ways. I have known several couples who gave up, got divorced and found life so tasteless without the invigoration of the struggle that they remarried and reestablished their exciting Peck Order conflict. Fighting may be miserable, but boredom can be worse. A few couples go through the divorce-and-remarriage cycle several times before they tire of paying attorneys' fees and decide that chronic warfare is cheaper than occasional settlements.

Couples vary in their techniques in Peck Order. Some maneuver with grace, and their elegant contest resembles a fencing match. Others pound each other clumsily, and their struggle resembles a tavern brawl. We shall now consider some of the more common maneuvers and stratagems used in Peck Order.

Screaming

Sheer noise is the most frequently employed maneuver in Peck Order. Shouting arguments, with or without cursing, are standard in most Peck Order stratagems. This maneuver usually accomplishes nothing for either party, since each person quickly becomes proficient in it and immune to it. The successful screamer skillfully picks the time and place to use this maneuver. Screaming which at home might cow neither person may carry the day when employed in a restaurant, at a cocktail party or in front of relatives. In recent years the outdoor patio has become a choice spot for well-timed Screaming since it can be heard easily by the neighbors. The successful strategist uses patio or restaurant Screaming if he knows that his opponent dreads public scenes and will give in quickly. However, the victory may be temporary. When Mr. and Mrs. Brown go inside from the patio or return home from the restaurant at 11:30 p.m., the defeated partner rallies in the kitchen or the bedroom and counterattacks with vigor. An exhilarating battle may go on all night as the defeated strategist regains his lost ground.

Home air conditioning has made Screaming a year-round maneuver. Thirty years ago, when home air conditioning was uncommon, house windows stayed open all summer and neighbors could hear the attacks and counterattacks whether or not it suited the immediate designs of the Peck Order contestants. Hence, Screaming tended to decrease in the summer and to increase during cooler weather. The advent of home air conditioning closed the windows all year long, and Screaming ceased to be a seasonal maneuver.

Guilt-Slinging

This is a favorite maneuver of Peck Order strategists; some of them develop great skill at it. The first step in skillful Guilt-Slinging is to examine your opponent carefully to discover choice vulnerable spots. Everybody has a few weaknesses, and careful study by a good Peck Order strategist can locate them. Then he begins the barrage of Guilt-Slinging, taking careful aim at the particular vulnerabilities of his opponent. For example, a man who did not get an expected promotion at work is open for a Guilt-Slinging stab such as "Look at this house and look at the way our kids are dressed. If you had buckled down on the job and not messed up the Burns-McDermott and Western Appliance accounts, you would have got that promotion instead of Ben Carter and we wouldn't have to be ashamed of this house and how our kids are dressed, and we wouldn't be in debt all the time." This maneuver usually gives the wife an advantage which keeps the man off-balance until he can find new weapons to use on her. Every time he tries to raise his bloody head, he gets bludgeoned again with the Burns-McDermott account and the Western Appliance deal. Many American business firms would be surprised to learn how useful they are to suburban housewives.

However, the husband can find good counter Guilt-Slinging maneuvers if he watches his opportunities carefully. For example, a bad purchase by his wife, especially if he advised against it, gives him an effective weapon. "Hell, if you didn't throw our money out the window all the time, we wouldn't have any financial problems. I told you to check that roofing company with the Better Business

Bureau before you let them put on a new roof for eight hundred dollars. I didn't like the smell of the deal. But, no, you thought you had a bargain. Look at the thing. A year old and it's already falling apart. Now I'm going to have to pay a couple of men to pull it all off and put a new one on. And if I've told you once, I've told you a thousand times, never buy anything from door-to-door salesmen. You paid one hundred seventy dollars for that vacuum cleaner and two months later Sears and Montgomery Ward both had the same damn thing on sale for a hundred and ten. What good does it do for me to make money when you throw it all out the window?"

The maneuvers of Guilt-Slinging are legion:

"I told you not to let Patty drive the car. Now we've got a two-hundred-dollar body-repair bill and they'll probably raise our insurance rates or cancel us out altogether."

"It seems to me a grown man ought not to be running over to his mother's house every time she whistles. You always have time to run right over there and put her storm windows up, but ours are still not up and it's the end of October, and the heating bills of this house are nothing to laugh at. You're always complaining about how I spend money and about how I keep this house looking. But, do I get a little cooperation from you? No. You're always over at your dear Mama's, and she has a hell of a lot more money to spend on her house than we do."

"Everybody gawked at you all evening while you were giggling and flirting like a teenager with that Fred Smith [or "that Mary Jo Wilson," when the wife uses this maneuver] at the cocktail party last night, and everyone thought you were ridiculous and repulsive. He [or she] is twice [or half] your age and you made a fool of yourself. He [or she] is no competition for me, but it's damn embarrassing to have you make a fool of yourself in public every time we go out and you have a couple of drinks."

We must not leave out the time-tested Guilt-Slinging theme: "If you didn't drink so much we would (a) not have so many debts and smashed fenders, (b) have more money because you'd be higher in the company by now, (c) have fewer problems with our children, (d) have a better sex life, (e) have smaller bills for liquor and our budget would be balanced, (f) still have all the friends we've lost because you quarreled with them when you were drunk, (g) have a happier home life because you'd get home on time," (h) other conclusions too numerous to mention in a book of this size.

Sexual Put-Offs

These maneuvers may be used by one or both Peck Order strategists. This thorny treadmill runs as follows:

"You shout at me all evening, and then you want me to get into bed, open up my legs and have sex with you. What do think I am, a cow? I'm not here to be kicked around all the time and then to hop into bed whenever you whistle."

"Sure, sure, baby doll, you bitch at me in public, tear me down all day long, and then want me to be a Casanova with you the next minute. Well, sweetheart, I've got news for you. I'm a human being, not a water faucet you can turn on and off whenever and however you damn please."

The variations on these themes are endless; they are an inexhaustible source of marital misery as the stratagems of Peck Order grind on.

Dragging in the Children

Some Peck Order strategists use techniques we have discussed in previous chapters. A common device is to drag in the children and to exploit them as cleverly as possible; a crying little girl or a cringing small boy may be a devastating foil in the hands of a good Peck Order strategist. Look What You Did to Our Child and That Awful Woman (discussed in Chapters 2 and 3) may be used in this manner. Torture Rack (see Chapter 2), used against both the husband and the children, is an excellent stratagem for a Peck Order player. Dragging in the Children makes Peck Order a very dirty stratagem which may have permanent unhealthy influences on their personality structures. Couples who conduct clean, sportsmanlike stratagems of Peck Order leave the children out. The finest stratagists define this clearly to the children with such comments as "Your father has his good points, but he's pigheaded and I have to keep him under control," or "Your mother is a good girl in some ways, but she's flighty and nervous and I have to straighten her out on a lot of things. In addition, she's too damn bossy for her own good or anybody else's."

Physical Force

This maneuver is sometimes employed in Peck Order. A surprisingly large number of "nice" suburban couples occasionally resort to slapping, punching, scratching, biting and hair-pulling. Such maneuvers are more common than is generally realized, since the participating parties do not advertise these activities to their friends and relatives. Punching and scratching are not socially acceptable in suburban circuits. When knowledge of such activities gets abroad in the neighborhood the couple's friends either demand they get divorced or, lacking that, drop them from their invitation lists. American marital (as well as premarital and extramarital) mores have been liberalized a lot in the last thirty years, but slugging, slapping and scratching are still not accepted. You can have sex with your neighbor's wife (or husband) while her husband (or his wife) is in Cleveland on business (or visiting her mother) and still stay on everybody's invitation list. However, if you pound your spouse, everybody drops you.

Physical Force usually occurs only in private, but a few brazen strategists use it in public. I recall a nice business-class couple in their thirties who one evening got into a bitter argument in a fashionable restaurant. The husband concluded the discussion by backhanding his wife across the mouth with all his strength, and she fell off her chair. As she climbed back up to the table he casually explained to his astonished friends, "She needs that once in a while." However, few couples can carry off such maneuvers with sufficient *savoir faire* to stay on invitation lists and country-club rosters.

George Is an Alcoholic, You Know

The stratagem of George Is an Alcoholic, You Know is executed by a subtly domineering woman who finds gratification in crippling her husband and then presenting herself as the brave little woman who carries on and raises the family despite the deplorable weaknesses of her alcoholic husband. The husband in many instances could remain sober, or at least function better socially and economically even while drinking heavily, if it were not for the camouflaged sabotage of his wife. This is basically a put-off stratagem, but it is so thickly tinted with come-on coloring that it actually may serve to hold a sick marriage together for decades or a lifetime.

The wife may get various gratifications from this stratagem. It allows her to be a brave little heroine in the eyes of friends and relatives. In many instances, the woman has profound needs to depreciate and dominate her husband; psychiatrists sometimes label her a "castrating female." After finding her husband's most vulnerable spot, she stabs and bleeds him while plaintively protesting that she is only trying to rehabilitate him.

This stratagem is well illustrated by Martha and George, a couple in their late thirties who had been involved in this stratagem for ten years. During the early years of their marriage the action of this stratagem had been desultory, but as George's business tensions increased and Martha's skill in the stratagem improved, it reached a pitch of higher intensity. The advent of their three children gave Martha three good foils for the fray.

George drank too much, especially when things were bad at the office. At first he drank only on weekends, but as Martha unconsciously learned how to devastate him with George Is an Alcoholic, You Know, his drinking spread out into the week. The pattern of the stratagem went as follows. George's drinking would get so bad that, despite the fact he was a top salesman, his sales manager would call him in and threaten to fire him if he didn't stop drinking. The sales manager would point out "your great little wife" and "three fine kids" as further reasons to "pull yourself together and lay off the stuff." Then he would call Martha, since everybody knew of Martha and her ten-year struggle to keep George sober, and would advise her sympathetically of what he had done while emphasizing that "the company just can't put up with this anymore."

Then George would take a cure. Usually he began attending Alcoholics Anonymous again, but twice he took Antabuse, a pill which prevents drinking by causing a severe physical reaction if a person drinks alcohol while taking the pill daily. Three times he had psychotherapy which began during a three-week hospital stay and continued on an office-call basis after he went home. The cure usually worked; George stopped drinking. His relatives were relieved, his sales manager was happy, and his wife beamed with approval.

Then, after about three months, his wife began another round of George Is an Alcoholic, You Know. She usually struck her first blow at a patio party or a gathering at the country club. When the subject of alcohol came up or when George refused a drink that was offered him and began to mutter something about its "not agreeing with my stomach," Martha stabbed in with, "George is an alcoholic, you know. He can't drink." As other people stared and tried to say something about the crab-grass problem or the greens committee of the country club, Martha followed up her attack with praise of George, "But George has been abstinent [a nice, cold, clinical word] for three months now, since he went back to A. A." At this point, George, squirming and wincing beneath the looks of the patio circle, would mutter, "Please, Martha, it's not important." Whereupon Martha would reply with enthusiastic vigor, "Oh, George, but it *is* important. Every alcoholic must recognize that he's an alcoholic and can't drink. He shouldn't be ashamed of it. That's the big step in winning the battle. We've both learned that from Alcoholics Anonymous and psychiatrists during the ten years we've been working to lick this problem. Haven't we, George?" George, red-faced and ashamed, would look pleadingly as he muttered, "Yes, Martha, but these people aren't interested in all this. Please, honey, drop it." Whereupon Martha would plunge on, seeing her victim already crumbling. "No, George, lots of people are interested. There are eight million chronic alcoholics in this country. And think of all the automobile accidents drinking causes. Remember the time you smashed up our Mustang, honey. But that's all over now. We've licked it, haven't we, sweetheart?"

This stabbing would increase in intensity for a couple of weeks as Martha continued to help George "fight the problem," while George's agitation, fury and rebellion rose. After about two weeks of George Is an Alcoholic, You Know, he would begin to drink again. This enabled Martha to move the stratagem into high gear, and she would rope other people into it. She would call Alcoholics Anonymous or George's doctor, and somehow or other she would let his sales manager know. The first morning George had a hangover and couldn't get to work on time, she'd call the sales manager and say, "George will be in a little late today, Mr. Gross. He's a little under the weather." As Mr. Gross hemmed and hawed, she would promptly admit that it was a "touch of the old trouble. But we'll lick it, since George has been doing so well lately." Mr. Gross would murmur something faintly encouraging as he apprehensively mentioned that the McNally account was hanging fire and they had to clinch it that week if they were not going to risk losing the account to the boys from the Tompson Company.

Thus armed with the McNally weapon, Martha would return to George, who was sitting on the edge of the bed drinking orange juice. (Without Martha's help he probably would have made it to the office by 10:30, complaining about being held up by a traffic jam behind a three-car pileup.) "You've got to pull yourself together, George. After all, you've got that crucial McNally account on your hands this week and everybody's counting on you." George would groan with despair since he knew she could have found out about the McNally account only by calling the sales manager that morning. Everyone in the office would know. The office girls would look up at him with curious sly glances as he came in, and the men would look at him with a mixture of solicitude and irritability. Mr. Gross would call him in and give him a pep talk about all that George owed to his family and "the company." He would hope ominously that he wouldn't be forced to turn the McNally account over to young Simpson "who really can't handle the situation as well as you can, but he's reliable." The word "reliable" usually made George's stomach fall four inches, reduced his self-confidence by fifty percent and increased his agitation by one hundred percent.

Within a week George would be drinking heavily again. Mr. Gross would be in despair (although the McNally account usually was clinched before George became incapacitated), and Martha would be overtly brave and undaunted, but unconsciously triumphant. Now they were all set for another "cure." This stratagem occurred in predictable cycles about three times each year. The heavy party season before Christmas usually ensured a relapse in December and a cure in January. I "cured" George in three Januaries in four successive years. Martha missed one January.

George Is an Alcoholic, You Know often is interminable. The

wife usually manages not to drive her husband into permanent dereliction, for this would end the exciting cycles of the stratagem and rob her of its main attraction, the periodic emasculation of her husband. Moreover, she would lose her comfortable upper-middle-class way of life with the patio parties and the country-club get-togethers. In the animal world a well-adjusted parasite never kills the host animal it infests; if it killed the host, both of them would die. A successful parasite lives on the host, bleeds him, weakens him, but never kills him. A woman who carries out a successful stratagem of George Is an Alcoholic, You Know skillfully follows the same pattern. Of course, occasionally she overplays the stratagem, forces her husband permanently into dereliction, and the stratagem ends. In most instances, however, the miserable cycles go on for decades.

We psychiatrists break up a few of these stratagems by treating the wives and the husbands, but we usually don't see these couples until the stratagem has been going on for five or ten years. By that time our roles are usually reduced to those of impotent spectators, or, worse still, we become the periodically employed tools of the wives to "cure" their husbands so that another round of the stratagem can start four months later. I usually bow out after the third go-round. Some stratagems are just too painful to watch. Moreover, my conscience bothers me about taking money from people when I know I'm really not solving their problems but simply have become incorporated into them.

This Poor Mistreated Girl

This is a three-handed stratagem played out by a young couple with marital troubles and a middle-aged man who ostensibly tries to help them but ends up destroying their marriage. The older man may be a family friend, a neighbor, an attorney or a professional person whose counsel they seek. Though he believes he is motivated by altruism, the middle-aged adviser is swept along by unconscious sexual attraction toward the young woman and by competitive hostility toward her husband. He becomes the vociferous protector of This Poor Mistreated Girl against That Awful Brute, her husband. The meddlesome counselor, often self-appointed, enjoys the role of protecting Dutch Uncle toward the girl and the indignant avenger toward her Awful Husband. Occasionally the unconscious sexual force behind his stratagem breaks forth to cause much turmoil to him and perhaps to the girl, but usually it remains camouflaged and is perceived by no one. In this stratagem the older man is swept along by unconscious come-on feelings toward the young woman and by put-off feelings toward the young man. He ends by destroying whatever come-on forces exist between the couple and creating strong put-off feelings in their place.

I recall a Poor Mistreated Girl threesome which consisted of a couple in their late twenties and a fifty-six-year-old businessman who was their next-door neighbor. The relatives of the young couple all lived in distant cities and the older couple acted as Dutch Uncle and Aunt to them. "Uncle Bob" and "Aunt Betty" grilled steaks for them on their patio, took their children to ball games and watched television with the young wife and her children in the evenings when the young man was out of town on business. It was a cozy situation and appropriate for a devastating threesome of This Poor Mistreated Girl.

In the course of time the young housewife, whom we shall hereafter refer to as Sweet Young Thing, talked over with Uncle Bob whatever marital differences she had with her husband, whom we shall hereafter refer to as Brutal Husband, although he was no different from most twenty-nine-year-old American husbands. Uncle Bob was full of sympathy and helpful suggestions. He assured Sweet Young Thing that he would talk to Brutal Husband and "straighten him out." He affectionately assured Sweet Young Thing that any man who had marital troubles with a "little angel" like her must be out of his mind, and that he, Uncle Bob, would correct these little problems. However, his officious, meddlesome lectures to Brutal Husband made things only worse, and Brutal Husband was angry with his wife for having discussed their personal problems with the neighbors. He felt uncomfortable and irritable with Uncle Bob and Aunt Betty and began to avoid them. Uncle Bob took it upon himself to correct this "surly attitude toward everybody," and their relationship deteriorated further. As the months went by Brutal Husband saw less of Uncle Bob and Aunt Betty while his wife became more dependent on their "helpful" counsel. As Uncle Bob sympathized with This Poor Mistreated Girl and "protected" her against That Awful Man, the marriage progressively degenerated.

Unfortunately, Uncle Bob had read a good deal about psychiatry in books for laymen, and he could fling the jargon around with debonair ease. He spoke of himself as Sweet Young Thing's "father figure" and said he was attempting to "preserve the ego structures" of Sweet Young Thing and her three children during this "marital crisis." He diagnosed Brutal Husband first as a "hostile personality," but later he discerned "sadistic and psychopathic features" in him. Uncle Bob questioned Sweet Young Thing carefully about what she knew of Brutal Husband's mother and then confidently declared that Brutal Husband "was acting out hostility toward his mother onto his wife." At this point Uncle Bob proclaimed that Brutal Husband was a "sick, sick man who needs help." He recommended long-term psychotherapy with a psychiatrist. The young husband exploded and told him that their main problem was his meddling in their marriage and that they had no big problems until they met him. Uncle Bob pointed out this "paranoid thinking and behavior" as further evidence of how "sick, sick, sick" Brutal Husband was. Sweet Young Thing clung closer to Uncle Bob and Aunt Betty as her marriage fell apart.

The young man begged his wife to break off with the older couple, and she sobbed that they were "the only ones who understand our problems." She implored him to do all that Uncle Bob suggested and to see the psychiatrist to be "cured." On two occasions in the heat of their arguments he slapped her, and he began to drink on weekends as his home disintegrated and he was powerless to stop the process. Uncle Bob further protected This Poor Mistreated Girl against "all this physical brutality and alcoholism." Eight more months of this stratagem led to a divorce court. Uncle Bob and Aunt Betty were the witnesses who helped This Poor Mistreated Girl to free herself from "this sick, brutal man who refused to accept help for his problems." Uncle Bob had carried out a good stratagem and had vanquished his rival. Everybody praised him for his altruistic help to Sweet Young Thing and her "three neglected children."

This grim stratagem sometimes has even more disastrous consequences. The older man's sexual attraction toward the young woman sometimes breaks through into his awareness and she sometimes develops a sexual infatuation for him. I recall a young couple who took their marital problems to a well-known clergyman for marriage counseling. The clergyman became involved in an intense stratagem of This Poor Mistreated Girl with the attractive young woman, who played her role with seductive charm and unconsciously enjoyed being the center of so much masculine concern. Within three months the clergyman and the girl were engaged in a sexual affair as he was swept along by his passions and by the girl's tearful begging for "all the warmth and strength I need so much and which only a good affectionate man can give me." The husband discovered the affair and revenged himself by a nasty divorce and child custody suit. Everybody lost heavily in this stratagem.

This Poor Mistreated Girl is dangerous for everybody concerned. Middle-aged men should stick to their golf and their wives and leave marriage counseling to the professionals.

Paranoia for Two

When a husband and a wife do not have love or harmonious companionship to hold their marriage together, they may devise interesting stratagems to keep their union intact. All these stratagems are miserable, but for the involved couple a miserable marriage may appear better than the loneliness, economic uncertainties and social desolation which they fear will follow divorce. Obviously, the stratagems they devise must depend on something besides love, since they do not love each other. These stratagems may depend on fear, hatred, pity, guilt, hostile competitiveness and other unhealthy emotions and may keep a marriage afloat for years, for decades or for a lifetime.

Paranoia for Two is an ingenious stratagem for keeping a loveless marriage going; it is a strong come-on stratagem which makes use of put-off pyrotechnics to accomplish its end. This stratagem was developed to a high state of efficiency by my patients Mr. and Mrs. Irwin. Two people less qualified for marriage to each other, or to anyone else, could scarcely be found. Mr. Irwin was an infantile, demanding, temper-tantrumish man who did not have close friendships with men or women. Mrs. Irwin was an insecure, frightened, dependent but explosively angry woman who was socially isolated. Mr. Irwin was sexually impotent most of the time and Mrs. Irwin was sexually frigid. How the Irwins managed to contrive a long-lasting marriage out of such materials makes a fascinating study. They did it by a superb stratagem of Paranoia for Two.

Their courtship was brief and fitful. In Mr. Irwin's travels over a large part of the country for an advertising company he periodically spent a week or ten days in the city where the future Mrs. Irwin lived. Both of them were lonely, isolated people. After a staccato courtship of weekend dating scattered over a period of several months, they abruptly married. They were both in their middle twenties.

On their honeymoon each one unconsciously discovered that he was uncomfortable with sex and did poorly at it. Rather than face up to this problem, they quickly fell into the maneuver of bickering endlessly over small points all evening long so they could go to bed peeved with each other and thus avoid the customary pace of honeymoon sexual calisthenics. Toward the end of the honeymoon Mr. Irwin slapped Mrs. Irwin at the height of an evening argument, and this relieved them of facing sex for three weeks.

Thus, the chronic battle of the Irwins began, and by virtue of their continual quarreling they sustained a vibrant, though turbulent, relationship in their marriage. Without this fighting, they would have drifted into silent isolation from each other, for if they didn't quarrel they could find nothing else to talk about. Incapable both of sexual passion and harmonious companionship, the only way they could sustain an intense relationship was to make a perpetual battleground of their marriage. Without it their marriage was a dreary wasteland of boredom and silence, and this frightened both of them badly and drove them out on the battlefield again. The prospect of separation and divorce devastated them. He dreaded the endless lonely nights in hotel rooms and she feared a return to the staleness of her life before marriage. Though the Irwins were not particularly happy in their marriage, they were not bored. There was plenty of commotion at all times.

After several months of marriage they began to develop what was to become the main bond between them, Paranoia for Two. Mrs. Irwin one night accused her husband of flirting with another woman at a party and neglecting her. Mr. Irwin flew into a rage and told her she was crazy. Mrs. Irwin thereupon exploded; she told him she had suspected him of infidelity for some time and that henceforth she was going to accompany him on all his out-of-town business trips. The ensuing argument lasted until 5 A.M.

After that Mrs. Irwin accompanied Mr. Irwin on all his business trips. She enlivened their travels with a continual sniping barrage about the way he looked at waitresses, receptionists, secretaries and shopgirls. Mr. Irwin remonstrated, ranted and sighed disgustedly; he said she was ruining his job. Mrs. Irwin complained continually of the inconvenience of having to travel with her husband all the time to keep him from extramarital affairs. Actually, each one dreaded solitude and preferred the companionship of traveling with the other.

Unexpected things began to happen. As Mrs. Irwin traveled with her husband, his income skyrocketed. She could type and she took over the paper work in his job. For two hours at lunch or dinner with a customer and his wife, they could hold themselves together, and people went away from these lunches and dinners much impressed by "that devoted, charming couple." Two years later Mr. Irwin became sales manager of his company at an income of $40,000 a year. All the good things of life followed—costly clothing, expensive automobiles, meals in the finest restaurants, afternoons in the most talked-of beauty salons, and all the other things that money and credit cards procure. Mr. Irwin's work required continual travel; hence, they bought the largest, most luxurious trailer home they could find and moved it from one city to another every two or three months. Their fights were the wonder and the consternation of the trailer courts they inhabited, and their fellow residents were diverted far into the night by her screaming and his curses.

As the years passed, their stratagem of Paranoia for Two became entrenched. Both of them now had more to lose in a divorce since each had become accustomed to the things their money was buying. As each one clung tighter to the marriage, their Paranoia for Two, which was all that held them together, became more intense. Mrs. Irwin opened her husband's mail and searched his pockets and suitcases for clandestine letters from paramours. She examined the glove compartment of their car for used condoms and inspected the upholstery of the car for what she called "love spots." Handkerchiefs and shirt collars were examined for lipstick stains, coat shoulders were examined for long blond hairs and face powder, and his underwear was diligently inspected for signs of illicit sex. Needless to say, an errant hair occasionally was found on a coat lapel, or a small stain of some sort was discovered on the car upholstery. This "conclusive evidence" spurred her on to new vigilance and cemented their relationship with violent quarrels for six weeks thereafter.

Meanwhile, Mr. Irwin began to reciprocate by accusing her of infidelities. He charged that all her suspiciousness was merely a cover-up for her own illicit behavior. He accused her of flirting with men and of clandestine meetings with her lovers. His customary vocabulary for her was enlarged to include such words as "slut," "whore," "prostitute," "tramp," and "shameless bitch in heat," and he charged that she was staying with him only for his money. He periodically announced he was leaving their trailer home for a four-hour business meeting and then returned without warning in forty-five minutes; he rushed into their home and searched it thoroughly, shouting, "Where is that son of a bitch? I know he's in here somewhere." On other occasions he would ransack the drawers and closets, throwing his wife's clothing all over the floor in a search for "sex stains" on her clothing and other vaguely defined evidence of marital infidelity. After four years of marriage, Paranoia for Two was well established and promised to enjoy a long run.

After twelve years of marriage they consulted me. They had already seen psychiatrists in New Orleans, Detroit and Atlanta. They both stated that each psychiatrist had reported that the other marital partner was "very disturbed." They both indicated that the only reason he or she did not seek divorce was because "I don't know what would happen to him [or her] if I left him [or her]. He [or she] would go to pieces." In each instance of psychiatric consultation they had seen the psychiatrist for about three months and then quit because, as each proclaimed, the other one "wasn't cooperating." Each one praised the psychiatrists as fine men who had failed because the other marital partner "hadn't cooperated." Their experience with me followed the pattern of their previous psychiatric contacts. Each one spent all his time, whether seen individually or jointly, recriminating and accusing the other. After three months they both canceled further appointments because the other one "wasn't trying" and thanked me for my good intentions. Two months later Mrs. Irwin reappeared to say that they were suing each other for divorce and that her husband had moved to a hotel. She said she wanted to see me for counseling while going through the divorce. Two days after that she canceled her next appointment, saying that they were now living together again and had dropped their divorce suits.

Ten years have elapsed since I last saw Mr. and Mrs. Irwin. However, about once every three years I get a letter from a psychiatrist in a distant city stating that they have consulted him and requesting a report on my opinions and treatment of them. Appropriate authorizations for release of professional information, signed by Mr. and Mrs. Irwin, accompany the letter which asks for help in "evaluating this difficult situation." The letters have come from Los Angeles, Pittsburgh and Nashville. It's about time I get another such inquiry.

Paranoia for Two strategists call in psychiatrists periodically. It makes the stratagem more respectable. However, they don't stick with a psychiatrist long, since breaking up the stratagem would deprive them of the only bond that holds them together and protects them from the wastelands of loneliness and boredom.

Stalemate

Stalemate is the most common dilemma encountered in marriages today. Stalemate does not consist of maneuvers and stratagems; it is a slow drifting into boredom which destroys a marriage so insidiously that neither marital partner knows what is happening. It is caused by perfunctory pecks on the cheek instead of passionate kisses, forgotten anniversaries and birthdays, hair that is always in curlers, sex that is wrestling instead of lovemaking, and a thousand forms of carelessness that never happened during the courtship but which begin after the honeymoon. Stalemate brings more misery to more marriages than all the maneuvers and stratagems of marriage lumped together.

Stalemate is produced by dropping all the romantic techniques of courtship at the altar. The man who held hands with his wife by the hour before their marriage now finds such handholding ridiculous. The man who kissed and caressed his future wife all evening long before the wedding now pecks her on the cheek and is annoyed if she expects anything more. Whereas birthdays and other special occasions brought telephone calls and flowers before marriage, he now forgets them entirely and is annoyed if his wife reminds him later. The man who prophesied the bliss of marriage before the wedding forgets to mention now that he has married the object of his dreams, and he rarely tells his wife he loves her. The man who enjoyed hearing his future wife talk endlessly during the courtship now snaps at her if she interrupts a television program to talk to him.

The wife similarly dumps her winsome wiles at the altar. The flowing tresses which stirred her husband's passion before marriage now are chronically bound up in hair curlers which make her head look like the body of a singed chicken. She who nestled her luxuriant hair against his cheek during courtship now stabs his face with hair curlers during sexual intercourse. The girl who was careful never to quarrel during courtship brawls during marriage. The woman who told her husband what a "dream" he was during dating now castigates him because he didn't cut the grass or bring home a bigger paycheck. Before marriage she thought he was "a magnificent specimen of a man"; after marriage she discovers that his hair is too thin at the temples and his waistline is too large, and she tells him so. The girl who before marriage enjoyed his putting his arm around her waist now pushes his hands away as she snaps, "Don't mess up my dress, and stop pawing me all the time."

Thus, romance drops out of the marriage, and the married couple drift into a dull, tasteless Stalemate. In many instances, neither marital partner realizes what is happening, and they may never realize it. Sometimes a wife realizes what is happening only when she discovers that her husband is having lunch every day with his secretary. The secretary is not bored by his conversation, never appears before him in hair curlers, and thinks he is handsome and wonderful. In other instances, a man is jolted into confrontation with Stalemate when he discovers that his wife is spending too much time with a fellow who belongs to their country club.

Many married couples spend very little time alone with each other. The treadmill of long working hours, bowling leagues, out-of-town travel, bridge luncheons, committee meetings, poolside parties and all the other distractions of the affluent life may leave the couple with little time in each other's company and even less time together alone. Stalemate can occur in any socioeconomic group, but it is particularly prone to occur in the suburban rat race.

Stalemate usually is soluble if the couple become articulately aware of their situation and devote intelligent work to resolving their problems. The people involved in Stalemate usually are fairly normal men and women. Their lives are not being distorted by maneuvers and stratagems, but by a careless drifting into indifference toward one another. Yet Stalemate is the most common disorder destroying marriages today. It probably causes more divorces than all the marital maneuvers and stratagems put together. The formula for breaking up a Stalemate is simple: Do in marriage what you did in courtship.

GENTLEMEN: Stare at your wives, especially when they are attractively dressed, or even attractively undressed. Every woman likes to be ogled by an admiring male, even when the male is her husband. Tell your wife she is good-looking, and pat her on the places you thrilled to touch before you married her. Make sex an interesting adventure, not a perfunctory set of calisthenics. Talk to her while you have sex with her, and tell her how wonderful she is. Remember her birthdays until she doesn't want to remember them, and then remember Valentine's Day and your wedding anniversary. Send her flowers unexpectedly once every three months, even though she protests that "we can't afford it"; divorce lawyers and alimony checks are much more expensive. Date your wife at least once a week; take her out for dinner to an Italian restaurant and ogle her across the spaghetti and cheap red wine. Slap her playfully on the bottom once in a while. She'll protest, "Oh, Ben, we're too old for that," but she'll not move away.

LADIES: Doll up a little before your husband comes home from work. Kiss him as he comes in the door. Don't hit him with the problems you had that day with the children until after dinner. Praise him for the big deals he makes and let his failures go by. After sex, tell him what a Casanova he is. They all like to hear it, and if he doesn't hear it from you there are always other girls waiting in line to tell him so. Make your complaints and quarrels brief, if you must have them; you can say all you have to say in two minutes, and after that it's only endless repetition. Then be affectionate again. In short, be a girlfriend to him all your married life. It pays. He'll be more generous, more faithful, more affectionate and a better husband.

Above all, ladies and gentlemen, spend some time with one another. The wife of a psychiatrist friend of mine once asked her husband, "How much time do you spend with a patient?"

"Fifty minutes."

"Do you realize," she said, "that between television, the newspaper and those medical journals you don't spend fifty minutes a day talking with me?"

The next evening the psychiatrist came home, mixed a couple of cocktails and called his wife into the family room. He glanced at his watch and they sat down to talk. At the end of fifty minutes he said, "Your fifty minutes is up," and he picked up his newspaper. Thereafter, he did this every evening either before or after dinner. This was an odd, mechanical way to go at the problem, but it was the beginning of breaking up a Stalemate.

6

Sexual Maneuvers and Stratagems

Sexuality, with its myriad forms of expression and sublimation, is one of the basic forces in human existence. Its action in human behavior is ubiquitous and constant. In its more obvious forms it leads to the formation of families and the creation of children, and in its less obvious forms it is intertwined in some manner, large or small, in almost all social and economic activities. No other emotional force in life leads to so much pleasure and so much agony. Sexuality is the strongest come-on force which operates in human relationships, but in the maneuvers and stratagems of people it may be distorted into an equally powerful put-off force.

The maneuvers and stratagems which people use in sexual relationships with each other are legion and extend from the mild maneuvers of a courtship squabble to the lifelong problems of a homosexual. In this chapter we shall consider a few sexual maneuvers and stratagems which show the ways sexuality radically affects premarital and marital interactions, family relationships, and the social and economic lives of people.

Straighten Up and Be a Man

This nasty little stratagem is played by a domineering woman who enjoys seeing a man squirm. The stratagem revolves around the man's sexual impotence; by carefully operating a good stratagem, a clever woman can reduce a formerly good man to complete sexual impotence and can derive many advantages by exploiting the inadequacy he feels in his relationship to her. Straighten Up and Be a Man is basically a put-off stratagem, but the man's feelings of inadequacy and shame may bind him to the woman in a distorted come-on manner.

Sexual capacity in a man is much affected both by his basic attitudes toward women and by his self-confidence in his masculinity. The man who fears women as engulfing, domineering tyrants is more prone to develop impotence than the man who views women with comfortable, affectionate self-confidence. The man who was endlessly berated and belittled by a domineering mother throughout his childhood is a more probable candidate for impotence than the man whose mother gave him an affectionate, sound relationship. The problems of the marital bed often begin in the nursery cradle.

Sexual prowess is important to the self-esteem of most men. Though a man may be a dignified judge, a captain of industry, a national golf champion or a distinguished physicist, he feels worthless and debased if he cannot perform an act which he shares in common with dogs, rabbits, cattle and rats. The most august man may cringe in shame at the sight of his wife on a bed sheet because he cannot perform a three-minute act which any alley tomcat can carry out. Impotence in men is common. In 1912 Sigmund Freud wrote an article on impotence in which he stated that, after anxiety states, emotionally caused impotence was the most common complaint of men seen in psychotherapeutic practice. Dr. Freud's article is still valid today.

Most men fail in the sex act from time to time, and many men go through periods of impotence lasting a few days or a few weeks and then recover. Anxiety, fatigue, a strange bedroom, coughing children in the next room and a hundred other factors can reduce a man to flaccid inactivity for one night or several weeks. I recall a Coast Guard medical corpsman who was so furious with his superior officer that he was in an agitated turmoil most of the time. Since he could not talk back to his persecuting superior, he seethed inwardly. When his puzzled wife asked him why he couldn't have intercourse with her at night, she was astounded to hear, "Because I just lie here and can't think of anything except how much I hate Lieutenant Willoughby." After a conference with his tearful wife and four sessions letting him explode his fury about Lieutenant Willoughby, the corpsman recovered his sexual power, and harmony returned to the marital couch.

Some women, however, exploit brief periods of impotence with diabolical cleverness; they castrate the man with cutting words and slicing depreciation. The woman then can watch him squirm in humiliated inferiority for weeks, months or decades. Such a woman often is skillful in getting fur coats, wall-to-wall carpeting, vacations in Acapulco, new cars and all the other good things of life out of her husband's impotence. "It's only fair that I have a few pleasures in life since so much is lacking in our marriage" is a powerful theme for carpeting houses, filling two-car garages with late models and putting fur stoles on closet coat hangers. A skillful Straighten Up and Be a Man strategist knows just the right innuendo to terrify her husband that she will expose him in confidential complaints to her girlfriends, who will then tell their husbands, who will then look upon him with scorn and condescending pity. Useful jabs by the wife are: "Well, you can at least provide me with a new car, since there's not much else you can do for me." "Of course, I know that none of my sisters has such an expensive home, but they have husbands who can give them satisfying marriages." The emphasis is on the word "satisfying."

Most of the women who carry out this stratagem do not like sex, or at least they are quite willing to trade it off for a houseful of expensive furniture and an open-ended checking account. Thus, in Straighten Up and Be a Man, the woman is trading off what is for her a worthless trifle in exchange for a big advantage over her husband; this is the cruel fraud of the stratagem. Though she protests that she is chronically miserable from lack of sex, she is secretly relieved to be rid of it. Moreover, she always resented the implied superiority of her husband in his being on top of her in the sex act and of the act's depending on his aggressive pursuit of her in bed.

The woman who operates this stratagem usually is skillful in picking the man she marries. She has an uncanny sense for noting a small thread of insecurity in a boyfriend's passion for her, and she unconsciously knows that after a few years of marriage this thread can be woven into a rope with which to control him. After they marry everything goes along well for a while; although the man may fumble and fail occasionally in sex, she says nothing and bides her time. Often she waits until the marriage is well sealed by two or three children. Then one night the husband fails to get an erection during love play, or he loses his erection just before or just after penetration. Now the wife begins Straighten Up and Be a Man. She demands, "Come on, Jim, don't leave me up in the air like this. I'm all excited and I've got to be satisfied." As Jim desperately tries to get himself aroused she slices in with further cuts which rob him of any possibility of regaining his erection. "What's wrong with you, Jim? Why get me all excited when you can't do anything? Don't tease me like this unless you're man enough to carry through and satisfy me. After all, you know how passionate I am and how much I need a man to satisfy me. Aren't you man enough to do what you're supposed to do? Straighten up and be a man. Maybe you should see a urologist to find out why you're not like other men." A judicious mixture of anger, agitation and tears, either in bed or after fleeing to the ostentatious seclusion of the bathroom, usually finishes poor Jim off.

After several such episodes the man approaches each episode of intercourse with fear of impending failure. He is robbed of any possibility of successful intercourse by the tense questions in his mind: "Will I or won't I tonight? Can I or can't I? What will Helen do if I don't make it?" Despite such anxiety he occasionally succeeds in intercourse, but the skillful Straighten Up and Be a Man strategist is prepared for such emergencies, and she complains, "Why do you get it over so fast and always leave me unsatisfied? Just in and out and get it over. Is that all you're good for now?" After a few months of such maneuvers the man often is impotent permanently, or at least he fails ninety percent of the time. The fur coat and wall-to-wall carpeting stage of the stratagem has now arrived.

Sometimes the stratagem takes a different turn, which the woman may be able to employ to her advantage. The desperate man may seek to solve his problem by sexual experience with another woman. The other woman may be a divorced or married girlfriend, or "one of the girls at the office," or a prostitute. Sometimes the man can do better sexually with a gentle, affectionate girlfriend who glosses over an occasional failure with "That's all right, honey. You're just tired tonight. We both know you're a big, strong man." However, the skillful wife who is carrying out Straighten Up and Be a Man has been watching out of the corner of her eye for just such an extramarital excursion. She now has a new weapon, Infidelity and Abandonment of Home and Children, with which to pound her husband. She "discovers" the affair and smears him with guilt over his neglect of her and his family because of "that little tramp at the office." She may have tearful scenes with her husband's mother in which she "accidentally" breaks down crying and can't resist her mother-in-law's entreaties to "tell me what's the matter, dear." This usually brings his mother's guilt-slinging down on the husband in addition to his wife's tearful tirades. He can't defend himself since he is too ashamed of his impotence to explain what drove him to another woman. The wife never lets him forget his brief extramarital peccadillo, and his misery and slavery are increased. Sometimes a descent into alcoholism both alleviates and complicates his misery.

However, sometimes the wife fails in this stratagem. The man may find self-confidence, affection and self-esteem on another mattress. He may break and run. He may divorce his wife and marry the other woman who doesn't play Straighten Up and Be a Man with him. He may see through his wife's stratagem when he can compare her behavior with that of another woman. He decamps, leaving the Straighten Up and Be a Man strategist with an empty bed and a monthly alimony check. Straighten Up and Be a Man is a risky stratagem; it is played for high stakes and the woman usually wins or loses a great deal. No man is completely predictable when he is desperate.

The Dolly Stratagem

This stratagem is worked by a coy, seductive woman who lures two men in pursuit of her and then plays them off against each other; she glories in the role of being the luscious prize for which they are fighting. This stratagem is employed by a self-centered, narcissistic woman who never loves any man, although she works this stratagem with many of them as the years and decades of her life roll by. Men are things to her; they ornament her like earrings or bracelets, and she never has more than a self-gratifying interest in them. After a few weeks or months she tires of the duo she is toying with and is ready to move on to another pair of victims. In some instances, a Dolly strategist executes brief, rapid Dolly maneuvers at cocktail parties and similar gatherings. She manages to allure two men and to set them glaring at each other within an hour after she enters the room. Then she moves on to find another couple of men on whom to execute the same maneuver, leaving the first two in ridiculous animosity in the corner. The Dolly stratagem is blatantly come-on in appearance but profoundly put-off in substance.

Other women can identify Dolly strategists easily and they unite in solid hostility against them. Men are slow to see through the Dolly stratagem or never see through it. Dolly strategists usually have no women friends, but they have a wide, superficial acquaintanceship with many men. No women are hated with such intensity by so many other women for such valid reasons as are Dolly strategists. An experienced observer of cocktail parties can spot a Dolly strategist with ease. She has the latest kind of eye makeup, her hairstyle is arresting, her dress is stylish and subtly tight in the right places, her smile is ready, her teeth are brightly white, she is always found talking charmingly with one or two men, and there are no women in her immediate environment. Careful survey of the room reveals one or two other women glaring at her from long or close range. Dolly's escort or husband is getting drunk at the bar, or standing stupidly by, or running after waiters to get more hors d'oeuvres for her and the men she is talking to. Thus, the Dolly strategist is quickly identified by her behavior and by the effects she has on the people around her.

Next, you observe her mode of operation. At first she concentrates on Man A. She finds his jokes uproarious, his observations penetrating and his accomplishments astonishing. She is brimful with girlish admiration for this big wonderful man who made two over par on the golf course yesterday or landed a big contract in Dallas last week. She leans heavily on his arm as her laughter at his witticisms convulses her so much that she temporarily needs this support, or she playfully brushes a stray hair from his lapel. After Man A has been carefully snared, Man B appears, and the circle of two becomes a circle of three. At first, Man A is proud to show off his charming admirer to Man B. However, his mood changes as he finds her attention shifting to Man B, who gets the same treatment he himself had been getting for the past hour. The contest between A and B for her attention becomes heated and Dolly finds both of them "tremendous guys." A and B alternate between bids for Dolly's attention and sniping hostility toward one another. A little bit of alcohol lubricates this machinery immensely.

As things come to a climax Dolly gracefully departs from the scene, leaving A and B frustrated, puzzled and angry at each other. She suddenly glides across the room to see a "dear old friend," or elopes to the ladies' powder room (the last best refuge of a woman in time of crisis), or abruptly discovers that her escort or husband is looking for her and decamps with her arm draped over his. A good Dolly strategist can repeat this sequence a couple of times during an evening party. A week-end get-together offers even more possibilities, and two weeks at a resort gives Dolly a wide field for action.

This stratagem can be extended to last a few weeks or several months, and the accumulating tension becomes explosive. When the Dolly stratagem is played for long periods, especially by married women, it also becomes risky. Men may have public arguments, or take shots at each other or at Dolly, or file for divorce, when a Dolly stratagem gets out of hand. A good Dolly strategist avoids such crises. She judges her men carefully and knows when to abandon the campaign by dumping one or both of them. She closes the chapter and then opens a new one with a new set of characters. In rare instances an unstable man threatens, rapes or abducts a Dolly strategist, and the result may vary from mock melodramatic to tragic. A man sometimes arrives at the "If I can't have you, nobody will" stage, and the situation may career wildly out of control. Dolly strategists themselves may make melodramatic suicidal gestures to throw everybody off-balance when the situation is deteriorating into chaos. However, these unhappy endings are uncommon. Dolly strategists usually carry off the campaign successfully or at least terminate the whole affair with relatively little damage to themselves. The havoc they inflict on other people's engagements and marriages is quite a different matter. Other women hate and fear the Dollies for valid reasons.

Dolly strategists may glide through two or three marriages as they pass through their twenties, thirties and forties, and I have seen a few strenuous Dollies who managed to get in and out of five or six marriages in two decades. They may scatter a few children along the way to be reared by former husbands or by the children's grandparents. Dolly usually finds children excess baggage as she careers along. Sometimes a Dolly manages to stick permanently in a marriage with a bumbling husband who passively goes along with his wife's social acrobatics while his friends regard him with amazed pity. "Why does Larry put up with Dolly's carrying on? I'd slug her or divorce her if she were my wife." Other Dolly strategists execute only brief one-night stands at cocktail parties, and although they annoy their husbands they never go so far as to threaten their marriages. Others carry out light, tantalizing Dolly maneuvers involving their husbands and party friends or acquaintances. When the Dolly stratagem begins to get a little hot Dolly flees to her husband's arms, reassures him of her undying affection and dumps the other man with the sudden observation that "my husband is insanely jealous."

Dolly stratagems may be carried out by women of all ages, including women in their sixties and seventies. Male vanity and susceptibility to female seduction wane only with physical invalidism or senile debility. Dolly stratagems played in middle age or thereafter flatter all parties concerned and rarely are dangerous. However, there are exceptions. I once had a sixty-five-year-old patient who was still carrying out Dolly stratagems and had her seventy-one-year-old boyfriend arrested when he tried to break down her apartment door because she refused to admit him late one night. Their children were perturbed by the scandal and the amorous activities of their presumably sedate parents.

I recall a twenty-seven-year-old Dolly strategist whose husband dragged her in for psychotherapy when he got tired of watching her continual maneuvering in this stratagem. As a rule, Dollies are difficult to treat, for although they are glib talkers, they do little more than spar with their psychiatrists. However, this Dolly gradually was able to explore her problems and could trace out some of the fantasies which lay behind her behavior. "You know," she said, "I think I imagine myself as the Dolly in every situation." She went on to explain that in all comic-book stories about adventures in outer space there is an attractive young lady dressed in a seductively tight space suit. Much of the action revolves around the attempts of the Bad Guys from another planet to kidnap this lascivious young lady and to carry her off to their hideaway on Mars or Saturn. This stock comic-book character, she said, is known as the Dolly. She is surrounded by a supporting cast which consists of the Hero, the Bad Guys, and a middle-aged scientist called Dr. Smith who assists the hero with the latest kinds of disintegration guns and death rays in his valiant struggle to protect the Dolly. "I guess I always imagined myself as a kind of Dolly in every situation, with men fighting over me," she concluded.

That is where I got the name of Dolly for this kind of stratagem.

Superman

A reasonably good capacity in sexual athletics is a significant factor in sustaining the vanity and self-esteem of most men. Despite the fact that, as we pointed out earlier in this chapter, august Homo sapiens shares this ability with animals ranging from donkeys to alley cats, most men feel that their intellectual capacities and professional skills are sadly tarnished if not coupled with this most common ability of the entire animal kingdom. However, in some men the need continually to demonstrate sexual prowess becomes a ruling obsession, and these men engage in the various maneuvers and stratagems of Superman. Sexuality is a powerful come-on emotional force, and the varieties of Superman are either caricatures or distortions of it.

The Supermen may be divided into two general subgroups: the Casanovas and the Frauds. The Casanovas, for one reason or another, are driven on an endless treadmill of sexual pursuit and on a moment's notice can deliver the bedroom performance that their dapper talk promises. The Frauds, however, execute an excellent seductive maneuver up to the bedroom door, but then quickly disappear when the time for performance arrives. The Casanovas have a sick need to perform; the Frauds cannot perform well, or perhaps they cannot perform at all, but they camouflage their problem with Superman talk and maneuvering. On the surface, it is difficult to tell the Casanovas from the Frauds on casual observation. However, there are some signs which are helpful, though not entirely reliable, and we shall consider some of them.

A Casanova may be tall and handsome or short and fat. He may dress in well-tailored suits or dirty work clothes. He is a good talker and he's always on the prowl. He has an acute eye for distinguishing seductive looks from indifferent stares. He knows all the double entendres, from the most subtle to the most obvious, and he is expert in all the stages of chitchat that lead from the barroom to the bedroom. He smiles a lot, laughs a lot, and, for a two- or three-hour stretch, he is a good companion. He is indiscriminate in his pursuit of single women, married women and divorced women, and race is no barrier to him. After he has passed the age of forty, he overlooks a woman's age in favor of performance and willingness, although in his twenties and thirties he is more selective. He usually is married and frequently has been divorced once or twice. He has two to four children scattered through a couple of marriages. In some instances he is married only once to an unsuspecting or resigned wife. He does not have much interest in sports or other avocations; he knows what his main preoccupation is, and he does not get distracted into other fields. He rarely puts his hands on women in public; he knows the right time and place for that. His sexual affairs are brief; they usually last only a few weeks, but they may last from one afternoon to several months. He is ready to execute his favorite maneuver morning, noon or night, and he knows from experience how to pick the girls who will perform from the girls who won't. He knows what is glossy glitter and what is yearning flesh, and he makes his selections accordingly. Casanova is always on a fast, restless treadmill of maneuvers and stratagems. Contrary to popular supposition, he is not a particularly happy man, and he is never satisfied.

The Frauds, who are completely or partially impotent and are engaged in an endless series of desperate maneuvers and stratagems to hide this fact from themselves and others, may seem similar to the Casanovas on superficial observation. However, the experienced party-watcher can distinguish them. The Fraud is a neat dresser and he is well groomed. He tries not to get fat and he covers his baldness with a hairpiece. He is more likely to be single than the Casanova. If he is married, his maneuvers are executed mainly when his wife is not present. She knows his secret and might explode and give it away if he flaunted Superman tactics in her face, especially after she has a few drinks. He is more apt to execute Superman maneuvers on out-of-town business trips and in other social situations into which his wife does not enter.

The Fraud, unlike the Casanova, talks a lot about sex in social groups; he is master of the obvious innuendo, the erotic pun and the hackneyed double entendre. The Casanova talks chitchat in the party room, mentions sex lightly to girls in quiet corners and is ready for bedroom action; the Fraud flaunts sex in the party room, avoids quiet talk with coy girls in corners, and never lets himself get caught in the bedroom. The Fraud flirts openly with the most attractive girls in the room, and avoids the plainer, quieter girls who actually may be more sexually available. He favors sexy banter with flirtatious girls who are ten to fifteen years younger than he is, and he shies away from women his own age or older.

He desperately seeks to present the spectacle of himself in hilarious, sexy banter with the most attractive girl in the room. The Fraud often has his arm over the back of a girl's chair or on her shoulder or around her waist; in his apparent passion he just can't keep his hands off her. Whereas Casanova settles down to work on one girl at a time, Fraud keeps up his lascivious banter with several of them. Fraud passes from girl to girl and from circle to circle as the evening goes on.

What makes Casanova run so hard? In short, he's looking for something he can never grasp. He is seeking a warm, intimate relationship with a woman, but he can't settle down to it when he finds it; he always goes away restless and unsatisfied. He seizes upon the most obvious aspect, the physical one, of a relationship with a woman, and he makes a caricature of it in his unending quest for the comfortable love which always eludes him. He is incapable of sustained companionship with a woman; he can go no further than mattress calisthenics. Some women who know him may understand this; his male friends never understand it. The men envy his adventures with women and marvel at his sexual marathons; they never guess the gnawing, subtle misery which lies behind it. Aging Casanovas are pathetic. Their trophies are useless to them and they know the chase is coming to an end without ever having grasped the prize.

The Fraud, on the other hand, is scared. He is scared of women, scared of sex and, above all, scared that other people will find it out. His sexy banter and melodramatic pursuit of gorgeous girls are empty maneuvers and stratagems to convince himself, as well as others, that he really *is* a Superman. The possible reasons why he is scared of women and sex are scattered throughout the second and third chapters of this book. The ropes which hobble a grown man usually are woven out of apron strings, and the problems of the marital bedroom begin in the nursery. Frauds are harmless; they enliven parties and provide the pyrotechnics that bring zest to weekend gatherings. A Fraud rarely hurts anybody; he moves too fast, keeps it all in public and makes his sallies brief. He is everybody's boyfriend and nobody's lover. Husbands may become annoyed, but they dimly sense they have nothing to fear. A few hot words occasionally fly, but nobody gets punched in the nose. Fraud's harmless maneuvers and stratagems go on for decades and provide endless distraction for a continually moving stream of people.

A special variety of Superman is the post-vasectomy phenomenon. Vasectomy is a simple contraceptive operation for men in which the small tubes which carry semen are cut by skin-deep incisions made just above the groin. Vasectomy usually is performed in the doctor's office, and the man returns home afterward. It is employed mainly by couples with three or more children who want contraception without bothering with pills or rubber paraphernalia. Most men who have vasectomies do not have adverse psychological reactions to the operation, but a few of them bounce into wild stratagems of Superman. Vasectomy in no way affects sexual performance, but for a few men it has a symbolic, castrating connotation which propels them into sexual marathons. By such sexual acrobatics the man tries to demonstrate to himself and others that he is still a prime sexual athlete. This only happens to one percent of men who have vasectomies, and even these men usually recover after a few months.

I recall a thirty-six-year-old junior executive who went into a post-vasectomy Superman reaction which led him into wild sexual adventures. He previously had seemed to be a tame, contented husband. His post-vasectomy reaction climaxed when his boss entered the man's office (which had the door unlocked!) and encountered him engaged in sexual intercourse with his secretary on top of the large mahogany desk. The office staff saw enough through the briefly opened door to necessitate firing Junior Executive on the spot. News of this unhappy event spread rapidly and precipitated considerable marital trouble between Junior Executive and his wife.

Fortunately, some fast explaining by his urologist and some supplementary counseling by me patched up the marriage.

Most vasectomized men restrict their little stratagems of Superman to the marital bedroom in their anxiousness to reassure themselves that they are "all right." However, a few of them need forewarning and loving, reassuring supervision by their wives in the postoperative period.

Maneuvers and Stratagems Used in Merchandising a Common Product

Most human services have a market if the right customer can be found and the product can be skillfully merchandised. Sex is no exception. The most obvious merchandising of sex is done by call girls and house prostitutes who are frankly selling sex on a cash-for-service basis. However, the amount of sex merchandising each year by these enterprising ladies constitutes only a small fraction of the gross national product in this field. If one considers how other groups of women merchandise sex, inflate the apparent value, escalate the price and then give the customer shoddy merchandise, one may conclude that the call girls and house prostitutes are perhaps the most honest, fairest dealers in this commodity. The call girls are at least running a straightforward business; they are not imposing nasty maneuvers and stratagems on gullible, cheated customers.

Sex may be merchandised both in marriage and outside it. A single girl may retail her favors in carefully calculated deals for jewelry, fashionable clothing, apartment rent and all the other good things of life. Vacations in Acapulco, Las Vegas or the Catskills may be paid for with bedroom services by enterprising girls. We are not here discussing affairs of passion or affectionate companionship; we are discussing shrewdly calculated deals by clever girls who know that a man with a checkbook is the one necessary instrument for securing the pleasant miscellanea of life.

Much ingenious merchandising of sex is carried out by women who are seeking job promotions or an easier work load in the office; this field is open to both single and married girls. The slightly tarnished, but much envied, distinction of being the boss's favorite goes along with this kind of merchandising. These girls package the product with "I'm dazzled by you, Mr. Wilson" looks, tight skirts, and slightly lascivious walk as they enter and leave the office. Walking out of the boss's office is an art in itself. They know how much stocking and leg attract the customer and how much more may disgust him. They never lose sight of the fact that the object is to sell the product, not to give it away. Anybody can give it away; it takes a skillful strategist to get a good price. Good maneuverers know how to pull away from a man with a smile that invites rather than rejects, and they know when to succumb and when to resist the boss's playful kisses. They know that hackneyed tactics such as sitting on the boss's lap cheapen the product; instead they arrange to be caught standing at the side of the desk or demurely posed beside a filing cabinet. They know that the best way to allow the first physical contact is faint resistance mixed with an inability to resist the charms of This Wonderful Man.

The girl who merchandises sex in the office knows the crucial maneuvers and stratagems for keeping other girls from getting access to the boss. They become skillful in the in-office fighting to keep attractive competitors in the typing pool and out of the executive suite, and they can spot a rival before the rival herself knows that she is one. These stratagems may go on for months, years or decades. I recall a dignified elderly gentleman, the head of a large educational institution, who for thirty-two years had sex two or three times each week in his office with his secretary; they never locked the door and never were surprised by an inopportune visitor. The girl, who was in her late fifties when the stratagem ended, had a pleasant sinecure and a nicely furnished apartment in return for her skillfully merchandised services. The mandatory retirement age of the educational institution broke up this stratagem.

Some girls carry out vicious stratagems with sex if they get hold of a customer who can be easily frightened and stampeded after the stratagem is well established. They unleash the pay-off maneuver with "I don't know if I can go on like this much longer. Lots of times I feel I'm going to lose control of myself and make a scene in the office," or "I can't stand all this much longer. Your wife and I are going to have to have a frank talk to decide which one of us should bow out." These maneuvers may stampede the right kind of customer into desperate gifts and concessions. Once he is scared and on the run, the man may be milked for all he's worth; however, the girl must be careful never to let him regain his balance. The married girl may execute the same maneuver with "I'm getting so confused and upset that I may lose control and break down and tell my husband. But he's so unpredictable when he's upset." These stratagems may be executed to special advantage when the man is a junior executive who is terrified that his superiors will discover his office sex and that this disclosure will spoil promotion possibilities.

Girls who execute this stratagem must know their victims well. Some men terminate the stratagem with "Hell, baby, you can't bulldoze me," whereas other men crumble and can be bled dry. A well-trapped coward can be kept squirming and exploited for decades. I know one married woman who parlayed this stratagem into an executive-level salary, stock options and a personal office with a thick carpet. She had in her hands a scared executive whose wife owned a controlling interest in the business. I also recall a smart little wife who figured out what was going on, went down to her husband's office and fired a secretary who was squeezing him dry. The husband was so relieved and grateful that he never mixed sex with business again.

Some women merchandise sex with astonishing audacity and

skill. I recall a middle-aged clothing merchant who took his secretary, a divorcée, along on a business trip. The first night out they went to bed and had sex. At the beginning of the sex act the man heard a loud, snapping noise, such as might have been produced by the snapping of a garter. After the sex act was over she told him that the noise was the breaking of her "second maidenhead," and that by breaking this "second maidenhead" he had violated her virginity. She convinced him of this despite the fact that she had an eight-year-old son by her previous marriage. In the following months she impressed upon the businessman that he had an obligation to marry her since he had violated her virginity by breaking her "second maidenhead." Amazing to relate, within a year he divorced his wife of twenty-five years and married his secretary. Their marriage was miserable, expensive and chaotic. This enterprising lady carried the stratagem of sex merchandising to the highest pinnacle of fraud; she parlayed a nonexistent article, her "second maidenhead," into marriage with a man with a six-figure income. I assure the incredulous reader that this case vignette is true; both these people were my patients years later.

Other women merchandise sex inside the boundaries of marriage. A commonly encountered sex strategist is the tearful wife who can't settle down to enjoy sex "so long as we are living in this awful apartment," or "until we move out of this terrible neighborhood," or "until we move back to Stamford." In similar ways sex may be bartered for new drapes, dishwashers and new furniture. Of course, many women banter playfully and half seriously for household appliances and other goodies but do not let such maneuvers spoil their sex life if they run into resistance. "If I'm a real, good, sexy girl tonight, will you break down and let me buy that new living-room chair we've been looking at?" This is acceptable wifely behavior if she doesn't insist on the sexual price tag. After all, sweet, good girls should be rewarded with special favors now and then.

One of the nastiest maneuvers for merchandising sex is Look How I Suffer to Satisfy You. In this maneuver the long-suffering strategist portrays sex as a painful sacrifice she makes to sate the brutal lust of her husband. She may proclaim that sex is physically painful for her (although no doctor can find an anatomical reason why it should be), or that her husband wants too much sex, or that he pushes it on her when she is "not ready" or "not in the mood" (although no time ever seems truly opportune for such women). The wife may claim that the husband never satisfies her and imputes the defect to him. He either "takes too long" or "finishes too quickly," but shortening or lengthening the sex act never locates the precise elusive time length that satisfies her. "There's something wrong with the way you do it," she complains, but she can't give him any hints about the right way to do it. "You don't warm me up first," she whines, but an hour or more of presex love play still does not raise her to the proper pitch of passion. However, the long-suffering wife goes along with sex in order to carry out her stratagem of Look How I Suffer to Satisfy You. Her object, of course, is to enhance the value of the product she is selling. She makes the buyer feel that he must indemnify her for all the misery she endures to keep him supplied with the merchandise. The payment for her twice-weekly sacrifices is carefully adjusted to the amount of sex she so painfully doles out. Debits and credits are entered in the ledger, and the wife is bookkeeper. A good bookkeeper can dominate the marriage by putting high prices on the product she is selling and crediting the husband with low values for the things with which he pays her. Payment may be made in both tangible and intangible ways. Tangible payments include household goods, clothing, late-model cars, and so forth. Intangible payments include dominance in family decisions, in child-rearing procedures, in choices of friends, in exclusion or inclusion of his relatives in their social circle, in acceptance or rejection of a job transfer to a city she does or does not like, and so forth. This stratagem illustrates clearly the business axiom that the right kind of merchandising can inflate the price of a product far beyond its reasonable worth.

The cruelest frauds in merchandising sex occur inside marriage, since the seller is purveying something at a high price that should be given free with warmth and pleasure. Sometimes the seller misjudges her customer. She may raise her prices and shove off shoddy merchandise on him. She may assume that she has a monopoly on the market and forget that there are other suppliers who can provide a much better product at half the price or at no price at all. The buyer may seek out another supplier and he may find he gets a finer product at a lower price from a more agreeable producer. He transfers his account permanently to the new supplier and the old supplier is left without a customer for her merchandise. She then must try to pay the monthly overhead with a meager alimony check.

Any kind of sex merchandising is a corruption and a fraud. Sex should bring men and women together in affection and secure intimacy. Selling it is a form of larceny in which both the robber and her victim suffer. Sexuality should be a strong, comfortable come-on force between a man and a woman. The woman who merchandises sex often discovers in the end that she has distorted it into a put-off force that is destroying her relationship with the man to whom she is linked.

The Ancient Greeks and I: Some Maneuvers and Stratagems Commonly Employed by Homosexuals

Homosexuality is not a stratagem, but homosexuals have a repertoire of maneuvers and stratagems they often employ as they struggle to adjust to their perversion. Most homosexuals are not well motivated to change their homosexuality to heterosexuality; they cling to their homosexuality in the same manner that heterosexual persons cling to their heterosexuality. However, the homosexual way of life carries with it special interpersonal problems, and the homosexual is prone to carry out special maneuvers and stratagems in trying to live more comfortably with his problem. For homosexuality is a sickness; it is not simply another way of living. We shall consider some of the special maneuvers and stratagems employed by homosexuals.

Superpeople

A common stratagem used by a homosexual in trying to become more comfortable with his perversion is to proclaim to himself, to other homosexuals and to occasional other people that homosexuals are a superior kind of people. He advocates that homosexuals have greater intellectual abilities, finer artistic sensibilities, more skillful physical talents and finer tastes in enjoying the pleasures of life. He fondly believes that homosexuals dress better, eat more discriminately, decorate their homes more tastefully, and, in short, constitute a superior group of people far advanced over the dull, commonplace heterosexuals. Even the name he applies to homosexuals reflects this idea; he calls them the "gay" people.

A homosexual man may achieve a superficial glitter in his dress, manners, conversation and living habits. This glitter is produced by the incorporation of unexpected feminine qualities into an apparently masculine pattern. However, the homosexual's inner turmoil, his confused sexual orientation, and the instability of his love affairs with a stream of fickle paramours usually rob him of the more stable kinds of judgment and taste which heterosexual persons often have. The claim of being a Superpeople is a self-deception which homosexuals employ with themselves and with other people in their attempts to live more comfortably with their emotional turmoil.

The incidence of various kinds of emotional disorders is greater in homosexuals than in the general population. The basic personality traumas which produced his homosexuality make him prone to develop anxiety states, depressiveness, certain psychosomatic problems and other emotional difficulties. His love affairs are not buttressed into permanency by legal sanction, social acceptance and the creation of a family, and hence these affairs often are fickle and turbulent. The infighting that homosexuals carry on in stealing one another's paramours creates a chaotic jungle behind the façade of urbane sophistication which they present to the world. Only the homosexuals and the psychiatrists who peer into their lives know the emptiness and chaos which often exist.

Superpeople is an empty stratagem; it is not an explanation or justification of homosexuality.

Everybody Is One

Another common homosexual stratagem is to claim that homosexuality is immensely common. About three percent of the adult population of both sexes is a homosexual, but I have never met a homosexual who would put *his* estimate at less than ten percent, and figures that homosexuals proffer go to up to fifty percent or better. In addition to this, they intimate that most of the important people in the world are homosexuals, including political leaders, prominent industrialists and distinguished artists. The fabrication of Everybody Is One is offered as justification that I Am One.

A cynical adage states that a research statistician can take any research team's data and work out a statistical proof that their project actually demonstrated what they wanted to prove. Everybody Is One is the homosexual's particular stratagem of statistical hocus-pocus.

All Great Men in History Were

A favorite maneuver of homosexuals is to claim that all the great men in history were homosexuals. This list usually reads like the pronouncing biographical section at the back of an unabridged dictionary. They claim that all Greek and Roman men were homosexual as well as most men in all other ancient civilizations that produced anything worthwhile. Homosexuals usually skip over the Dark Ages in these selections, and expand the list immensely in the Late Middle Ages and the Renaissance. According to this point of view, the Renaissance was produced mainly by homosexuals, and all art and literature since then have continued in this tradition. The list goes on to include most military leaders, statesmen and scientists.

The kernel of fact in all this rationalizing is that homosexuality was openly accepted in Greek and Roman times and perhaps was somewhat more common than at present. The references to homosexuality in the writings of these times are frank, but it is difficult to know just how common homosexuality was. It is probable that the vast bulk of the population has always been heterosexual and that the maneuver All Great Men in History Were is executed by reading unjustifiable meanings into a great deal of the world's literature and art. However, the maneuver is an attractive one for homosexuals since no one can prove it's false. The ancient Greeks didn't keep statistics.

I'm Really Only Twenty-Five Percent Queer

A comforting stratagem that a homosexual may play is to compartmentalize himself and to believe that he has both a homosexual self and a heterosexual self neatly locked up in separate airtight compartments in his personality structure. He proclaims that he dons either personality by opening the proper compartment and adopting for a while the behavior pattern he finds inside. This stratagem leads to much misery for homosexuals and others.

A large number of homosexual men make occasional forays into heterosexuality, and a sizable percentage of them marry. However, they often continue homosexual liaisons during married life, and their marriages frequently end in divorce, leaving distraught wives and upset children behind. The marriages of homosexuals in middle age have a better chance of survival since middle-aged homosexuals finds themselves deserted by their youthful paramours and discover crushing loneliness closing in about them. They then may reach out for companionship with middle-aged women, but the incidence of serious marital trouble and divorce is still much greater than average.

A certain amount of mutual masturbation is common among adolescent boys and a few brief homosexual experiments in a man's life may be included within normal limits. However, the man who settles down to a homosexual pattern and lives in the homosexual community that exists in every large city is a homosexual. He can deceive himself only for a brief time, although often he can deceive others for a longer period. I'm Really Only Twenty-Five Percent Queer is a dangerous stratagem. Lots of people can be hurt in it, and sometimes they are hurt badly. To misquote both Gertrude Stein and William Shakespeare, "A rose is a rose is a rose, and to call it something else usually leads to chaos."

Cure Me If You Can

Psychiatrists differ in opinion about whether homosexuals are good candidates to change their sexual orientation in psychotherapy. Most psychiatrists feel that change from homosexuality to heterosexuality is accomplished infrequently in psychotherapy, and that it occurs only in strongly motivated homosexuals. Certainly, only a fraction of one percent of homosexuals enter psychotherapy and persist in it to the conclusion of becoming heterosexual. However, homosexuals frequently see psychiatrists for other psychiatric problems such as anxiety states, depressions and psychosomatic problems. In psychotherapy some homosexuals employ the stratagem of Cure Me If You Can, and if you can't then I'll settle down to what I am. They come for psychotherapy for a while with the feeling that if they are not "cured" they can continue their homosexual pattern with the comforting feeling that "I couldn't be changed, so I will settle down without compunction to being a homosexual." Such patients, needless to say, never (using the word "never" in the psychiatric sense, which means "well, hardly ever") make significant progress in psychotherapy. It's a stratagem, not a treatment situation.

7

∗∘∗———∗∘∗———∗∘∗

Business and Professional
Maneuvers and Stratagems

In the preceding chapters of this book we have dealt with the maneuvers and stratagems which are carried out in the intimate relationships of life, such as family relationships. In this chapter we shall describe some maneuvers and stratagems that are executed in broader interpersonal fields such as relationships in business and professional groups.

As we pass from the stratagems of the intimate relationships of life to those of broader social groups, we leave the strictly defined boundaries of psychiatry and move into fields where sociology and psychiatry merge. However, we are still dealing with fundamental human feelings such as hostility, fear, love, and desires to dominate other people or to be dependent on them. The basic field is still the same—the interpersonal relationships of people.

May the Best Man Win

This stratagem is executed in any kind of business, professional or governmental organization in which there is a hierarchy of authority, prestige and income. It is an increasingly common stratagem in our society as business, professional and government organizations tend to become bigger and more complex. As corner grocery stores fade and supermarket chains grow, as small companies are absorbed into bigger ones, as government proliferates, as professional services become organized into group practice rather than solo practice, as research increasingly is done by large teams rather than single persons, new maneuvers and stratagems spring up in the relationships of the people grouped together.

May the Best Man Win is the stratagem *par excellence* of business, professional or government hierarchies. It is a pure put-off stratagem based on the familiar human forces of ambition, greed, fear and the search for prestige and security. Its basic theme is that in the endless struggles that go on in business and professional hierarchies, the skillful strategist is careful to hire or advance not the best man but the man who least threatens the strategist's position.

We shall cite an example of May the Best Man Win. Strategist A is head of a company division or a government bureau or a research group. He must choose one of two men, B or C, as his second in command of the group. Sometimes, however, he does not actually make the choice. The choice is made by people above him, who consist of his superiors, a board of directors or a committee. But Strategist A has much to say about who will be chosen, and often the committee above him sees Men B and C mainly through his eyes because he can control to a large extent the information about B and C that reaches the committee. He writes reports about them, and he talks about them, and he organizes their work assignments in such a way as to make them appear in a productive or nonproductive light.

Let us consider Men B and C. B is the more capable of the two. He organizes things better, he gets more work done, he is brighter, and he makes a better impression. He knows more about the job, its problems and its possibilities. From an objective point of view, he is the obvious choice. But in Strategist A's eyes, he has an enormous drawback. As A's second in command, B would threaten A's position. A is fifty-three and B is thirty-six. As second in command, B would have direct access to the ruling board or committee. His capabilities would be obvious and his productivity easily noticed. Once he was firmly established as second in command he would be a formidable rival to A in any conflict or competition between the two of them. A has children to put through college, an expensive home in the suburbs which requires another eight years of payments, and an expensive way of life. To be brief, A knows that B is the best man, but B frightens him. B threatens A's security. With B well trained as second in command, A could easily be replaced by B. A no longer would be an indispensable man to the business section, the government bureau or the research group.

Now let us consider C. He is a diligent mediocrity. He does his job, but he needs A to keep him out of trouble. He is not a good administrator, but he can work well enough if he has a good administrator over him. He does not have A's knowledge and ability, and this is clear to everyone who works with him for a while. C is genial and easygoing. He clings to A since he needs him to get along reasonably well in his job. In short, C could not replace A as head of the group, although he could function tolerably well as second in command so long as A was there to guide him. Thus, C does not threaten A's job security. With C as second in command, A is an indispensable man. If A can keep his organization full of men like C and weed out all the more capable men like B, he remains a secure, indispensable person. The committee, the board of directors or the superiors above him say, "What would we do without A? We don't have anyone else who could carry out his job. He's a valuable man, and valuable men are hard to find." Hence, A gets raises, stock options, and prestige, and he sleeps well at night in his nice suburban house.

If A is an able strategist in May the Best Man Win, C gets the job and the threatening B is gently but skillfully edged out of the company during the next year or two. Actually, the Best Man is A, since he promotes C and gets rid of B; although the stratagem is called May the Best Man Win, the contest really is between A and B, not between B and C as a naïve observer might think. A good strategist in May the Best Man Win is not satisfied merely with promoting men like C; he weeds out men like B and fills the ranks with men like C who do not threaten his position. How does he do this? Listen well, you ambitious, frightened, clever little men who increasingly run the world, and I'll tell you how it's done. We'll list the steps by number.

1. Carefully prevent contacts between Mr. B and all the people who are above the two of you. Keep his desk at the far end of the office. Don't put him on committees that deal with your superiors and never send him to represent you when you can't attend to something yourself; send a C type of man. Don't let his name appear on reports of his work; mix his sales record or his production record with those of other men and report the total as the "Department Production Record for April." Then sign your name to it. This exploits B's productivity and you get the credit for it; this maneuver is an art in itself and many reputations have been made by mastering it. However, this maneuver is slightly risky because one of your superiors accidentally may discover that much of the department's work is being done by Mr. B. In this way, B may become too firmly entrenched for you to get rid of him. Moreover, you may find that you need him to meet the monthly production quota, and then you are in a jam. Your job security demands that you get rid of him, yet your job security also demands that you keep him. Ulcers are made of stuff like that. B may cease to pull your cart and he may want to climb up on the driver's seat. Careful strategists do not like such risks, but sometimes they are forced to take them, since too many C-type people may reduce departmental production to the point where A's leadership and organizational ability are questioned. As you can see, this stratagem is more complicated than it might first appear.

2. Carefully undermine B by mixing faint praise with strong

condemnation. This task may be carried out with statements such as (a) "B is a good salesman so long as he can keep his alcoholic problem under control. I've talked to him about it and I feel sorry for his wife, Betty. She's a fine, sweet girl." (b) "B could be one of our best men if he didn't have so much trouble with women. He just can't keep his hands off the girls in the office and the customers' receptionists. I've warned him about it, and I hope he snaps out of it. Lucille is his third wife, you know, and the kids of his first two marriages are with his former wives in Detroit and New Orleans." (c) "B would be one of our better workers if he could control his temper," or (d) "if he were not so shy and ill at ease with people," or (e) "if other people liked him better and could work with him." These points are repeatedly impressed on the committee until it appears that B's "problem" prohibits advancement in the company or perhaps even requires that he leave. A long, careful buildup puts A in position to fire B when an appropriate issue arises or when the job force is to be cut.

3. Get rid of B by eliminating his job in the hierarchy or by cutting the budget of the section he is in. In the name of "economy," or "careful cost accounting," or "changes to adjust to altered sales emphasis," or "changes owing to a shifting market," or "changing work loads," B's job often can be abolished. He then is given a glowing letter of recommendation, a big smile, a big regret, two months' salary, and he is terminated. This maneuver sometimes can be carried out simply by juggling the company organizational chart on the wall and eliminating a few boxes with names in them. Work is shifted from one desk to another or from one end of the office to the other, and in the process B is pushed out. Careful paper shuffling and renaming of the same activities frequently can accomplish the same objective. However, this must be done before B is firmly entrenched in the company. A good May the Best Man Win strategist can pick out the Bs when they are still low in the hierarchy and can eliminate them early, leaving lots of room for the Cs to grow.

4. Annoy B to death. For example, if B can't stand working with Miss Pennypacker, a longtime company employee who by meticulous plodding has risen to a position of limited authority, put B to work with Miss Pennypacker. She is a spinster bookkeeper who now runs a division of the accounting department, and she is a whining termigant who humiliates her co-workers. After six months with Miss Pennypacker, B resigns when A tells him he cannot be shifted to another job. When B goes, A sighs, "B couldn't even work with Miss Pennypacker, and she's been with the company for twenty-three years."

A can harass B in many other ways. He can criticize his failures in front of the office staff and ignore his successes. He can send all his reports back to be rewritten three or four times to include obscure red-pencil corrections in the margins or "to conform with company policy." When B asks what the company policy is on this point, A can reply, "B, do you mean to tell me you've been here three and a half years and don't know yet what company policy on this matter is? Go back and read the operations manual again."

A can put B's desk in the noisiest, draftiest, dirtiest place in the building. He can give him the most inept secretaries, delay all his supplies, and demand results without giving him the material with which to produce them. There are thousands of these minor but devastating techniques of harassment and A knows them all if he is a good strategist in May the Best Man Win.

5. Provoke B into a misstep and then fire him. If B has a temper, A should discover his vulnerable spots and can then harass him to the point where he blows up at A in the office or walks out of the office in a rage during the end-of-the-month rush period when his services are mandatory. One or two such blowups may make it easy to fire him.

6. Schedule B's work so as to make him appear unproductive. A can give him the jobs at which everyone else has failed, or he can assign him the customers no one else could sell. A can give him projects that require two years and demand that they must be

completed "on time" in six months. After a year or two of this, B usually can be eased out because "he just couldn't get the work done and wasn't carrying his share of the load."

7. Play a couple of Bs off against each other. Take two ambitious, eager Bs and give them conflicting jobs, overlapping responsibilities and sharp competitive roles. Then gently encourage each one to feel that you are backing him against the other. Unless they're very smart, they'll fall for the bait and cut each other's throats. Then you can get rid of both of them.

8. Exploit B's weaknesses carefully, viciously and systematically. If his weakness is women, give him the divorced, sexy office siren for a secretary and then fire him because of the ensuing "scandal." If his weakness is alcohol, send him to the conventions where heavy drinking is sure to occur. If his weakness is gambling, send him to deal with the customers who play poker for high stakes. These are vicious maneuvers, but when a man has a house in the suburbs to lose, kids to put through Ivy League colleges, country-club dues to pay and an expensive, nagging wife to support, he can be driven to the vilest of tricks and can find rationalizations to cover them.

Of course, despite all this, A doesn't always win. B may be too clever, or too obviously capable, or too tough to be eliminated. Sometimes B disguises his abilities behind flattery of A and frequently states, "I wouldn't get anything done without your help and guidance, Mr. A," while sabotaging A behind his back. B sometimes wins and in time he may grab A's place. Then B becomes A. However, there are many other bright, eager Bs coming along behind him. As Sophocles wrote, "For surely as all life is run, unto him that doeth it shall be done." May the Best Man Win again.

The Research Stratagem

Research is one of the dominant concepts of our time. Having originated in the sciences, the research concept has spread into most fields of activity. Commerce, industry, government, education and many kinds of institutions lean heavily on research in deciding future action and solving problems. However, like most human activities, research can be turned into a stratagem. In fact, the corruption of research called the research stratagem is spreading rampantly.

True research is a path to knowledge and the solution of problems. The research stratagem, on the other hand, is an end in itself whose main purpose is to sustain the research workers in a comfortable way of life. A research stratagem involves a mixture of come-on and put-off forces. The come-on forces exist between the members of a team of research strategists who band together in united larceny. However, in terms of the long-range welfare of society as a whole, these are basically put-off stratagems since they distract large amounts of money, talent and effort from valid attempts to solve the problems of business organizations, social groups, scientific institutions and government agencies. A secondary goal of the research stratagem is to sustain itself, extend itself and perpetuate itself. The subject being studied is a minor consideration.

Four factors make the research stratagem possible. The first factor is the huge amount of money now available for research. When large amounts of money are available and people are invited to apply for it, strategists always gather. The huge philanthropic foundations, the government and industry have large amounts of money to pour into research each year. The basic human forces in the research stratagem are the familiar ones—greed, the lust for prestige, the savor of power and, the eternal goal of a good strategist, the delicious fraud of something for nothing or at least something in return for minimal effort.

The second factor that creates a vast field for research strategists is that much of their work is not supervised by the people who hand out the money. The foundations or the government make large grants and often require only periodic reports. A good research strategist writes good reports, filled with obscure erudition and impressive statistics, and he can easily fill this requirement.

A third factor is that the people handing out the money often are not experts in the field of the strategist's work or at least in his aspect of it. Hence, they are not on sure ground in evaluating what he has done with the money.

A fourth factor is that the people who hand out the money are loath to admit to their governing boards and committees, "We made a mistake when we gave Dr. Smith and his team all that money for that silly project." Hence, the people who hand out the money often become co-conspirators in the research stratagem, although they may not know it. The people who give out the money praise the work and results of the recipients, and the recipients praise the foresight of the givers in financing their research. The board of trustees basks in the pleasant glory of having helped humanity, when the only thing that occurred was much rushing around and filling up lots of paper with printer's ink. Hence, the people who hand out the money usually choose a "safe, established investigator" who will not rock the boat or disturb the stratagem. The safe investigator has good credentials, sticks to well-trodden paths of investigation and writes good reports. Usually he is repeating work that has been done a dozen times before, but he always "is looking at the material from a fresh point of view" or is "examining it with a new research tool which promises to shed new light on this puzzling problem." His reports subtly praise the wisdom of the people who gave him the money.

An identifying characteristic of the research stratagem is that it is self-perpetuating and self-expanding. Every study concludes that "this study has revealed the need for exploration of wide new fields. The way is now prepared for solution of the problems we have been approaching [approaching, always, but never reaching]. We now have the knowledge and methodology [this word is worth millions] to proceed . . ." and so forth. So each study concludes with a request for more funds for another two or three years to "study the problem." The request is made in such a way that all preceding work seems lost if the study is not extended to reach the goal which is always just within grasp if more money is provided. In this way the professional research strategist boxes the foundation, the governmental office or whoever else gave him money, into giving him more. A good research strategist is like the proverbial tar baby; the more contact you have with him, the more you become stuck to him.

Another characteristic of the research stratagem is that it proliferates. The "team" grows; it puts forth little shoots that become big limbs and casts forth little acorns which grow into mighty oaks, and these oaks throw out even more acorns (Ph.D. type of acorns). Let us examine the process.

Dr. Green is an excellent strategist in the research field. He occupies the entire third floor of a university campus building with impressive offices untidily stacked with papers of all kinds, a computer, lots of earnest young men and women with horn-rimmed spectacles (budding strategists) and lots of graduate students who are subsidized out of research grants (infant strategists). These students are raised academically in the research stratagem and never even know it is a stratagem. If the stratagem is in a biological field there is a maze of test tubes and glassware strewn on formica-topped tables.

Dr. Green has all the marks of a good research strategist. He is out of town attending scientific or professional conventions half the time. He is on the editorial board of one or two journals in his field. He publishes half a dozen articles a year, in conjunction with three or four junior members of his team; no one is sure just who does the work or who writes the papers. No one is sure just who reads them. The foundation or one of the foundations which supply funds to him also subsidizes the publication of his books, so that "this valuable information can reach the limited professional audience toward which it is directed." The books otherwise would not be published, since nobody reads them and no publisher will print them without a subsidy. Dr. Green is the master of the editor type book. He gets together seventeen papers from a section meeting of a convention, he writes a preface and an introductory chapter, and he publishes the seventeen papers with himself listed as editor of the book. The book carries his name prominently in the introductory pages and lists all the other seventeen contributors on a single page later on. In this way Dr. Green can publish a book every year. Complimentary copies of these books are given to all the people who give him research money, and these people are impressed by all these pages of print. If anyone ever dares to question whether Dr. Green is worth all the money that is being poured into him, his defenders exclaim, "But look at the twelve books he has produced," and that squelches the opposition for eight more years. Note carefully that he "produced" these books; he didn't "write" them. If the opposition persists in questioning Dr. Green's contribution, the hapless skeptic is told, "Well, I wish you'd read the twelve books Dr. Green has produced and the seventy-six scientific papers his team has written, and then if you still feel his work is not valuable, we can go into this further."

Of course, Dr. Green has the book reviews of his books to display to doubters. The reviews are favorable; they are full of such phrases as "valuable contribution," "fresh point of view," "we are all grateful that this book was written," "should be on the bookshelf of every worker in this field," "we can recommend highly," and all the other clichés of book reviewers who skim through books but do not read them. The reviews are written by friends, colleagues, and former students of Dr. Green. Many of them also are research strategists who expect Dr. Green to review *their* books favorably. The reviews are published in journals edited by Dr. Green's fellow strategists, and Dr. Green is on the editorial board of one or two journals which have ten pages of book reviews every month. For skeptics, ten or fifteen glowing reviews of each of Dr. Green's books can be produced.

Even if some persistent skeptic tries to read Dr. Green's books to evaluate whether he is worth all the money that has been poured into him, he runs into a stone wall, for Dr. Green is a master of one of the prime requirements of a good research strategist; he writes excellent jargonese. He has mastered the use of the technical word in so esoteric a context that it is incomprehensible. He knows how to take a common English work and give it a new technical twist that confounds the unwary reader. He coins a new word now and then "to express a new concept for which we do not have an adequate term at present." Frequently he refers back to his previously published papers and books where the exhausted reader may "learn the concepts and terminology which are a necessary background for thorough comprehension of this material." Thus, anyone who complains about the jargon is referred back to a swamp of reading material as the way to understand Dr. Green's work, and this material in turn refers the reader to still other work of Dr. Green's fellow strategists, co-conspirators and predecessors. The skeptic is left feeling like a dunce because he hasn't read all this material or can't understand it if he has read it.

Dr. Green also is a master of the grammatical skills of jargonese. He never uses such things as vigorous verbs, stark nouns and brief sentences. He is a master of the inverted sentence, the passive verb, the dangling participle, the modifying clause, the indistinct subject and the vague predicate. He uses commas and parentheses with such skill that his sentences wander on endlessly until the reader forgets the subject of the sentence by the time he arrives at the middle of the predicate. If anyone objects that Dr. Green is hard to read and might write better, the imprudent upstart is crushed with the observation that "Dr. Green's work has to be studied, not skimmed through, and understanding it requires a certain amount of background, you know."

After fifteen to twenty years of this, Dr. Green is an "authority." He now can get all the money he wants for any project, since a foundation or a government bureau never can be criticized for giving a six-figure research grant to so distinguished an investigator as Dr. Green. Foundation people dread being asked, "Why did you make a grant to that young Montgomery fellow who is not an established investigator? What has he produced? What are his credentials? Don't you know that grants like that cause criticism of foundations? After all, this money is a public trust and we are responsible not only to our board of directors but to the community at large. Really, Jones, do you think you used good judgment in making this grant?" Jones has a house in the suburbs and three children with the sniffles who will have to go to graduate school someday, so he doesn't make any more grants to bright, original, probably creative applicants who are not well established in the research stratagem.

Dr. Green proliferates. His students go off to other universities and set up new research stratagems. They quote Dr. Green's articles and redo all the work he did twenty years ago, which was a repetition of someone else's work twenty years before that. In time a network of Dr. Green's former students has sprung up all over the country. They write chapters for each other's books, publish each other's articles in the journals they edit, praise each other's papers at conventions, vote each other onto committees, secretaryships and presidencies of technical societies, and finally give testimonial dinners to each other praising "lifetimes of accomplishment." All this is financed by excellent salaries (because "you've got to pay well to get good men"), generous expense accounts for conventions, and all the fringe benefits of the good research life.

However, every stratagem has its pitfalls, and one of the pitfalls of the research stratagem is that the strategists often do not know they are carrying out a stratagem. They were professionally raised in the research stratagem and accepted it as a way of life without questioning it. After ten years in the research stratagem they develop such a large vested interest in it that they cannot afford to disbelieve it. This gives the stratagem a certain risk. The strategist may become convinced that he actually *is* a "great man" and he may barge ahead too boldly in this role. He becomes dependent on the adulation, the prominence and the empty business of the stratagem. Sometimes, in middle age or later, the house of cards begins to fall. Some of the strategists' students may become skeptical, observant colleagues may become disillusioned, and his sources of money lose interest in his particular field and divert their money into other spheres of activity. His ability to execute a bright, dashing stratagem declines as he gets older. He also may go out of fashion; research, like other things, has its fads. But our strategist has become dependent on the daily adulation, the importance of being a "great man," and the endless round of committee meetings, conferences, out-of-town travel and conventions. As the stratagem collapses, the strategist becomes a peevish, bitter middle-aged man or an elderly has-been whom students ridicule and colleagues ignore. Some strategists carry the stratagem out brilliantly and successfully to the end, but others find that a bitter decline awaits them as they enter the last third of their course. The true scientist and the valid intellectual have their intellectual resources to sustain them. The strategist has only the glitter of his stratagem, and if this begins to crumble he has nothing left.

The Company Stratagem

The company stratagem is one of the common stratagems carried out in business and industrial organizations today. It is fueled by put-off forces in the strategist which disrupt interpersonal relationships in the company as he ambitiously propels himself toward success. In this stratagem, the strategist uses devotion to the company to mask his own ruthlessness in climbing up the company's hierarchy. The company stratagem is a kind of business or industrial patriotism, and, as Dr. Samuel Johnson observed, "Patriotism is the last refuge of a scoundrel."

The company strategist may be any age. He may be the bright

junior executive in his twenties who parades the glories of the company to his older superiors in flattering them about their accomplishments. He may be the deft salesman in his thirties who cuts the throats both of his fellow salesman within the company and of his competitors outside it "in the best interests of the company." He may be an executive in his forties who uses devotion to the company to cover his brutal policies of demoting, transferring and firing long-term personnel who are inconvenient to his personal goals and his desire to build a personal fortress in the company out of his favorites and the people who serve him best. As he fires or demotes a man, his theme is: "You know, Bill, this is the last thing in the world I want to do, but the company's interests demand it." He may be the executive or plant manager in his fifties who uses dedication to the company to get rid of younger men who threaten his position. Finally, he may be the executive or plant manager in his sixties who uses his long record of "devotion to the company" to prevent the board of directors or his superiors from retiring him before the mandatory retirement age. The strategist uses devotion to the company to mask every selfish, brutal move he makes in his upward progress through the ranks. Just as a Greek or Roman general used his apparent devotion to the gods as justification for his most brutal acts, the company strategist uses the new deity of the company to camouflage his ruthlessness and callous ambition.

Another characteristic of the company strategist is that the greatest part of his social life is spent with people who work for the company. He prefers social activities with his superiors or people on his own level, but he may throw a once-a-year picnic "for the girls in the office and their husbands." The company strategist golfs with company people, parties with company people, visits with company people, and lives in the suburb in which the most influential company members live. He invites them to dinner, gets invited back, cocktails them and gets cocktailed in return. His children go to the same schools to which a number of company families send their children. His wife makes friends with the wives of company officials, and she visits them, coffees them, plays bridge with them, shops with them and parties with them. Everybody cuddles in the collective security and bliss of the company.

The company strategist is adept with first names and promptly gets to a first-name basis with his equals and superiors. He refers to all company executives as "Bill," "Harry," "Dave," or "Todd." He has a wide first-name knowledge of company personnel in other cities, and he is an accomplished name-dropper in the casual manner. When another member asks, "Do you know Mr. Thompson who runs the Milwaukee office?" he replies, "Old Ben Thompson? Why, I used to play golf with Ben every Sunday morning for years. Ben always had a slice in his drives, but he made it up with his putting. I remember one time on the twelfth hole at Fairlawn when . . ."

The company strategist is a tireless purveyor of anecdotes about other company members, especially executives with whom he has hobnobbed. "I remember the time I was sitting with Phil Lerner in the airport lounge in Baltimore, and Ted Watts and Marty Nast from the Los Angeles office walked in. Well, Ted and Marty were supposed to be in Fort Worth that week working on the Peterson-Cartwright contract . . ." He knows endless humorous anecdotes about the wives, children, friends and dogs of important people in the company, and many of these stories subtly underline the close associations that *his* wife and children have with those company officials and their families.

The company strategist is an accomplished talker about big deals the company made, successful products the company developed and important contracts it obtained. In most of these stories his own name and those of other company officials are connected in prominent, seemingly casual ways. His favorite theme is: "We won despite the enormous odds against us." "I remember when Jerry Martin and I were sitting in a hotel room in Denver, gloomy as hell because we figured the Central Star deal was lost. Jerry said to me . . ." In fact, so many of his stories center on "how we won when all the odds were against us" that casual observers may conclude that he is the company's ace troubleshooter, which, of course, is the desired effect of these anecdotes.

The company strategist has a sharp eye for who is on the way up and who is on the way down in the company, and he shifts his friendships and alliances accordingly. The people on the way up are "Bill," "Tom" and "Dick" to him, whereas the people on the way down are "old Johnson" and "poor old Gardner, I like him in spite of the way he gets things balled up." The good strategist's wife shifts her friendships with equal skill and rapidity.

The company strategist is an expert at camouflaged flattery. He never tells the boss how great he is; he is too deft for that. Instead, he finds out what the boss' accomplishments in the company have been and praises them lavishly, discovering to his surprise that the boss had a role in them. "Well, if you ask me, the most significant development in this company in the last ten years has been expansion into direct consumer selling. . . . Why, Bill, I didn't realize you had so much to do with that development. Hell, you never talk about what you've done for this company." The good strategist also knows his boss' prejudices. He knows of the long-standing rivalry between the boss and Tim Wilson who runs the Pittsburgh plant, and he shakes his head as he says, "If they could only get that Pittsburgh operation up to the level of the rest of the company, it would make it a lot easier for the rest of us." If the boss is a bad golfer and a good bridge player, the strategist remarks, "Anyone who wants to take the time to hack it out can become a fairly good golfer, but a game like bridge takes brains." When the boss complains of someone in the company, the strategist sighs resignedly, "Yes, there are a lot of problems in that department. I've tried to talk to Sam about it, but it doesn't seem to lead to anything." The strategist agrees that the boss' enemies all are stagnating the company and that his favorites are all good company men who are helping to keep the company afloat despite the dead weight of the others. The boss soon concludes that the strategist is a "good judge of men."

Another characteristic of the company strategist is the rapidity with which he develops intense company patriotism. From the day he enters the company, his patriotism for it is instant and obvious. "This is just the kind of outfit you can really get interested in and work like hell for. . . . I feel at home here already. Everyone's been simply great to Marie and me in this company since we came to town." Along with patriotism for the company, he develops instant hostility toward its competitors, and he takes over company attitudes, company policies and company customs immediately. Like a chameleon, he promptly acquires the color of his environment. If he transfers five years later to another company for a better position, he develops a new patriotism with equal facility.

One of the strategist's main weapons is "company policy." The greatest injustices, the most callous cruelties, and the most blatant selfishness are justified by company policy. The strategist often is aided by the vagueness or the absence of clear company policy on many issues. Company policy then becomes a set of oral precepts passed down the ranks and vaguely justified by past actions. Company policy gives the strategist a cudgel to use against other people, both inside and outside the company. People are hired, fired, transferred, demoted, promoted, worried into ulcers, harassed into resignation, cheated, duped, deceived, bullied, flattered and evaded in the name of company policy. Whatever the strategist wants for himself is justified in the name of company policy, and whatever he does not want is evaded with the same mystic phrase. Company policy is hard to combat; if you fight it you are disloyal, especially in comparison to the loyal man who is using it against you. If you disagree with company policy you are questioning the wisdom of company officials, while the man who is employing company policy to further his own ends is allied with them. If you rebel against company policy, you lack patriotism for the company, and the strategist clubs you to death with company policy.

However, the company stratagem has its dangers; the worst one is retirement. When he retires at sixty-five, the company strategist at one blow loses the social life, conversation, preoccupations and avocations that for years or decades centered on the company and its personnel. His contemporaries in the company have retired, and they are scattered over the country. Once he has retired, the younger men in the company quickly lose interest in him; he is out of step with them and useless to them. Retired company strategists often become anxious, depressed, and self-concerned. They see doctors for exhaustive laboratory studies of obscure physical complaints. They sell their houses in the suburbs and move to apartments where they are miserable. The company strategist often lacks the flexibility to adjust well in retirement. In psychiatric practice I have seen more than my share of these unhappy men. The ancient Greeks believed in Nemesis, an inexorable force of retribution which paid to every man the just deserts, good or bad, of his acts. They felt that Destiny was a moral bookkeeper who settled his accounts with each man before the man died. In the end, the company stratagem often becomes a nemesis stratagem.

The Philanthropy Stratagem

One of the characteristics of our society is the profusion with which philanthropy is dispensed to large numbers of people from both private and governmental sources. When money is being handed out on a large scale, strategists inevitably accumulate. The philanthropy strategists corrupt philanthropy from its original purposes into stratagems whose main goal is the comfort and security of the strategists themselves. One of the factors which facilitate stratagems in philanthropy is that the givers are not giving away their own money. They are professional administrators who give away money that comes from private foundations or from the government. When people give away their own money, fewer stratagems occur. Philanthropy stratagems usually are come-on stratagems in their short-range effects. They bind the professional administrators of the philanthropic project together in their common goal of exploiting the philanthropy for their own welfare. In many instances the recipients of the philanthropy also are included in the conspiracy. However, the long-range results of philanthropy stratagems are put-off since they damage the true interpersonal needs of society as a whole.

Host and Parasite is a common philanthropic stratagem. In biology, a good parasite, such as an intestinal worm, lives off his host animal but does not kill him. Some parasites, such as certain intestinal bacteria, even perform useful biochemical functions for the host. In these instances, the host animal and the parasite have a mutually sustaining relationship. In Host and Parasite philanthropic stratagems the administrator who hands out the money and the recipient of it evolve a mutually sustaining relationship which ensures both of them long-term economic security. The giver unconsciously guarantees that he will provide money and other services to the recipient, and the recipient unconsciously guarantees that he will continue to be a valid recipient for an indefinite period of time. He will be a "worthy recipient" who never betrays the giver by improper behavior. He will be a "hopeful case" who attends treatment sessions faithfully but never gets well, or a rehabilitation trainee who is always "on the road to rehabilitation" but never arrives there, or a vocational trainee who is always "making good progress" but never becomes employable.

Many years ago I worked in a clinic which provided psychiatric services to a group of persons who received monthly checks from the government. This clinic was run by professional administrators with social-service backgrounds. I was one of various persons who "treated" our "clients," as they were called. The continuance of the clients' monthly checks was dependent on periodic reports we wrote affirming that they were still partially or totally disabled but still working to "solve their problems." Most of these persons had, by fits and starts, been attending the clinic for several years or longer, and the clinic had become self-perpetuating. It supported the small staff of professional administrators who talked to the clients' relatives, interviewed the clients and kept voluminous records on them. The clinic also provided supplementary income to a flow of young psychiatrists who remained with the clinic on a part-time basis for a year or two and then were replaced by other young psychiatrists.

After working in this clinic for a while I became impressed with the stability of the patient load. Few patients ever dropped out of treatment, and only a few patients from time to time were added to its rolls. The staff of the clinic had regular conferences to evaluate the clients' "progress," to discuss their "psychodynamics," and to outline "new steps to help them." The staff filled the clients' records with regular notes about their "progress," but their disability checks remained the same, and almost none of them got well. If one of the young psychiatrists suggested that a patient was not "making progress," the rest of the clinic staff were shocked at the young psychiatrist's "hostile feelings toward the patient." The senior psychiatrist who came in twice a week for case conferences analyzed the young psychiatrist's "negative transference" toward the patient and then explained that it was easy to become hostile and deprecating toward patients whom we could not cure quickly. He then discussed how the young psychiatrist's hostile feelings toward the patients were causing him to reject the patients and to want to punish them by reducing their monthly disability checks. This emotional problem in the therapist, the senior psychiatrist went on, was damaging to the patients. During this dissection of the young psychiatrist's "hostile, punitive feelings toward the patients" the longtime administrative staff of the clinic looked on with a glow of triumph. The conference usually ended with a subtle recommendation that the young psychiatrist needed treatment to rid himself of his "hostile, negative transference" to the patients. After such a session with the senior psychiatric consultant in front of the whole staff, the young psychiatrist usually sank into docility and became part of the philanthropy stratagem for the rest of the year or two he worked in the clinic.

However, sometimes a young psychiatrist persisted in his objections. Sometimes he pointed out that a patient had been attending the clinic for five or six years and that careful study of his record showed that his symptoms and general condition were the same as when he started despite continued notations about his "progress" and endlessly repetitious interviews. The young psychiatrist might even go so far as to suggest that since the patient was not changing, it would be much cheaper for the government simply to give him his monthly check, reevaluate him for disability once every six months and discontinue all this expensive treatment which was not really changing him. Some misguided young psychiatrist might even commit the unforgivable heresy of suggesting that it might be interesting to see if reduction of the patient's monthly check would spur him into taking some steps on his own. This always brought the clinic roof down on the young psychiatrist's head. The professional staff looked on with horror at the callous young psychiatrist who wanted to "leave the patient economically destitute and to abandon him to a lifetime of misery with his symptoms and no hope of relief through treatment." The senior psychiatric consultant took a much more serious view of the young psychiatrist. If the patient was older than the young psychiatrist, the consultant wondered if the young psychiatrist was "acting out his hostile feelings toward his father on this patient who obviously is a father figure to him." If the patient was female, the consultant commented on "hostile transferences toward mother figures" or the "hostility which arises when the therapist has erotic feelings which he cannot satisfy toward a female patient." A young psychiatrist who didn't immediately fall into line after such a thrashing elicited concerned comments about whether he had chosen his specialty carefully and whether perhaps he would be "more comfortable" in dermatology or anesthesiology.

This philanthropy stratagem went on from one year to the next, with patients and staff comfortably supporting each other. Needless to say, there was a provision in the budget of the clinic which paid the expenses of each full-time staff member to a national professional convention each year to "keep up with the latest developments in helping the patients." After nearly a decade in the same building, the clinic was transferred to its own section in a new government office building.

A group of skillful strategists can make a philanthropy stratagem out of almost any kind of philanthropic situation. One of their favorite techniques is to conduct a Study to determine how best to plan a philanthropy. I know one Study that has been going on for ten years. The Study is always preparing for a "program of action" which is continually delayed "until we have the information necessary to make realistic plans to help these people." The Study began with a three-year grant from two large foundations to examine the problems of a particular group of unfortunate people. At the end of three years a comprehensive report was to be made outlining a program of action to help these people. A ten-person team of sociologists, psychologists and social workers was brought in from other cities, and consultants were hired in statistics, psychiatry and internal medicine. Within a year, twenty people were working in this organization.

Much office space was occupied and the amount of paper work that went on was impressive. The staff interviewed people, analyzed the interviews, and made maps of the city which were filled with colored pins to show where the interviewed people lived. Newspapers interviewed the members of the Study group and published their pictures in Sunday papers. Members of the Study gave luncheon talks to women's clubs, university groups and business associations to "interest the community in the problems being studied."

At the end of three years a four-hundred-page report was made. The conclusion of this report was that the Study was coming along fabulously well, that all sorts of vital things had been discovered, and that the grant had to be renewed for another two years to finish it up. If anyone objected, the crushing reply was made, "Surely, after putting all this money and professional time into the Study, you don't want to abandon it when we're nearly at the end." The annihilated skeptic would mutter, "Well, we really do want to know what to do to help all these poor people," and the Study was liberally financed for another two years.

Books have been written about the Study, and a never-stopping trickle of graduate students in the social sciences have been supported on their roads to Ph.D.s by it. The personnel of the Study continually changes, except for a hard core of administrative staff who stick with it. One secretary is pointed out with awe to newcomers as a person who "has been with the Study since it began." The staff stay one to five years and then go on to good academic positions or to other studies. Hence, none of the people who finally analyze the data actually collected it. Many of the people who analyze the data have never seen any of the people they are analyzing. As yet no program has been evolved to help the poor people who are being studied.

The only thing that has continuity is the Study itself. It has become a self-perpetuating stratagem, and as each group of strategists go off to academic jobs or other studies, they are replaced by new strategists. The foundation administrators who support the Study are loath to drop it and to admit to their boards of directors that it never reached its objectives and that they poured so much money into so profitless a project. The stratagem has supported, fed, clothed, conventioned, and professionally boosted many happy strategists.

How will this stratagem end? Elementary, my dear reader. After about fifteen years all the persons who were board members of the foundations when the Study began will have died or will have retired. At some skillfully chosen point, the Study will be officially closed. A huge report will be written. It will be ornamented by many pages of colored graphs and charts, and the length of the appendix alone will terrify all readers out of reading it. The report will cite all the books and papers written about the Study, whose publication, incidentally, was paid for out of Study funds. The report will name all the participants, with their Ph.D.s after their names. The Study will be termed a huge success, a monument of social progress and a "turning point" in civic planning.

But how will the strategists get around the nasty question about what is to be done for all the poor people who were to benefit from the program evolved by the Study? This difficulty is solved in a simple manner. The report grandly points out that all the necessary information is now available to help these people, and it sends the reader off to the library to read all the articles and books spawned by the Study. It makes no difference that the books do not agree with one another (this will be called "lighting up various facets of the problem") and that the conclusions of the articles are confused and contradictory (this will be called "showing the complexity of the problem and that no single answer fits all aspects of it"). Moreover, it would take a year to read all this material, and much of it is unreadable. In addition, anyone who read it would not find anyone else with whom to discuss it since no one else has read it all. Then, our report grandly concludes, all this material is leading to great action. It implies that city planners and welfare organizations receive their daily inspiration from the light shed by this Study. In short, we are dazzled to learn that the Study was a glorious success. Meanwhile, back in the slums things go on as before, and the benighted citizens of these regions are ungratefully unaware of how much they have been helped.

It takes an expert observer to distinguish valid philanthropy which helps the recipients from philanthropy stratagems which help the strategists. The philanthropy stratagem can be carried out in the arts, in educational institutions, in rehabilitation institutes, in welfare groups and, in short, in every part of the broad spectrum of altruism. Worst of all, the vast majority of philanthropy strategists do not know they are carrying out stratagems, and a person who thinks he is devoted to helping his fellowman is a formidable person, even when he is executing a meaningless stratagem which he does not understand and in which he has a vested interest because it supports him.

Circumlocution Maneuvers and Stratagems

Maneuvers and stratagems are not new. Observant people have studied them for centuries, although they did not call them by these names. One of the most astute students of maneuvers and stratagems was Charles Dickens, and one of Dickens' classic descriptions of a stratagem occurs in his novel *Little Dorrit,* where he discusses the workings of a mythical department of the British government called the Circumlocution Office. Dickens' description of this department was so poignant that several divisions of the British government complained that he was attacking them. Although written over a century ago, his description of the colossal stratagem executed by the Circumlocution Office is still a valid description of stratagems employed today in government, in business and in institutions. We shall let Dickens describe this stratagem himself; we cannot make his comments more contemporary by rephrasing them.*

* Throughout this selection I have changed six words to give it more cogent meaning for modern American readers. These changes are: "gunpowder plot" is changed to "plot to blow up Congress," "Oxford Street" to "Pennsylvania Avenue," "Parliament" to "Congress," and the words "premier," "Barnacle" and "lords" to "statesmen." About twenty other words have been omitted entirely. In all other respects the selection remains as Dickens wrote it in 1855.

CONTAINING THE WHOLE SCIENCE
OF GOVERNMENT

The Circumlocution Office was (as everybody knows without being told) the most important Department under Government. No public business of any kind could possibly be done at any time, without the acquiescence of the Circumlocution Office. Its finger was in the largest public pie, and in the smallest public tart. It was equally impossible to do the plainest right and to undo the plainest wrong without the express authority of the Circumlocution Office. If a plot to blow up Congress had been discovered half an hour before the lighting of the match, nobody would have been justified in saving Congress until there had been half a score of boards, half a bushel of minutes, several sacks of official memoranda, and a family-vault full of ungrammatical correspondence, on the part of the Circumlocution Office.

This glorious establishment had been early in the field, when the one sublime principle involving the difficult art of governing a country was first distinctly revealed to statesmen. It had been foremost to study that bright revelation, and to carry its shining influence through the whole of official proceedings. Whatever was required to be done, the Circumlocution Office was beforehand with all the public departments in the art of perceiving—HOW NOT TO DO IT.

Through this delicate perception, through the tact with which it invariably seized it, and through the genius with which it always acted on it, the Circumlocution Office has risen to overtop all the public departments; and the public condition had risen to be—what it was.

It is true that How not to do it was the great study and object of all public departments and professional politicians all round the Circumlocution Office. It is true that every new statesman and every new government, coming in because they had upheld a certain thing as necessary to be done, were no sooner come in than

169

they applied their utmost faculties to discovering How not to do it. It is true that from the moment when a general election was over, every returned man who had been raving on hustings because it hadn't been done, and who had been asking the friends of the honorable gentleman in the opposite interest on pain of impeachment to tell him why it hadn't been done, and who had been asserting that it must be done, and who had been pledging himself that it should be done, began to devise, How it was not to be done. It is true that the debates of both Houses of Congress the whole session through, uniformly tended to protracted deliberation, How not to do it. It is true that the speech at the opening of each session virtually said, Gentlemen, you have a considerable stroke of work to do, and you will please to retire to your respective chambers, and discuss, How not to do it. It is true that the speech, at the close of each session, virtually said, Gentlemen, you have through several laborious months been considering with great loyalty and patriotism, How not to do it, and you have found out; and with the blessing of Providence upon the harvest (natural, not political), I now dismiss you. All this is true, but the Circumlocution Office went beyond it.

Because the Circumlocution Office went on mechanically, every day, keeping this wonderful, all-sufficient wheel of statesmanship, How not to do it, in motion. Because the Circumlocution Office was down upon any ill-advised public servant who was going to do it, or who appeared to be by any surprising accident in remote danger of doing it, with a minute, and a memorandum, and a letter of instructions, that extinguished him. It was this spirit of efficiency in the Circumlocution Office that had gradually led to its having something to do with everything. Mechanicians, natural philosophers, soldiers, sailors, petitioners, people with grievances, people who wanted to prevent grievances, people who wanted to redress grievances, people who couldn't get rewarded for merit, and people who couldn't get punished for demerit, were all indiscriminately turned up under the paper of the Circumlocution Office.

Numbers of people were lost in the Circumlocution Office. Unfortunates with wrongs, or with projects for the general welfare (and they had better have wrongs at first, than have taken that bitter recipe for certainly getting them), who in the slow lapse of time and agony had passed safely through other public departments; who, according to rule, had been bullied in this, overreached by that, and evaded by the other; got referred at last to the Circumlocution Office, and never reappeared in the light of day. Boards sat upon them, secretaries minuted upon them, commissioners gabbled about them, clerks registered, entered, checked and ticked them off, and they melted away. In short, all the business of the country went through the Circumlocution Office, except the business that never came out of it; and *its* name was Legion.

Sometimes, angry spirits attacked the Circumlocution Office. Sometimes, Congressional questions were asked about it, and even Congressional motions were made or threatened about it, by demagogues so low and ignorant as to hold that the real recipe of government was, How to do it. Then would the right honorable gentleman, in whose department it was to defend the Circumlocution Office, make a regular field day of the occasion. Then would he come down to that house with a slap on the table, and meet the honorable gentleman foot to foot. Then would he be there to tell that honorable gentleman that the Circumlocution Office not only was blameless in the matter, but was commendable in this matter, was extollable to the skies in this matter. Then would he be there to tell that honorable gentleman that, although the Circumlocution Office was invariably right and wholly right, it was never so right as in this matter. Then would he be there to tell that honorable gentleman that it would have been more to his honor, more to his credit, more to his good taste, more to his good sense, more to half the dictionary of commonplaces, if he had left the Circumlocution Office alone, and never approached the matter. Then would he keep one eye upon a coach or a crammer from the Circumlocution Office and smash the honorable gentleman with the Circumlocution Office account of this matter. And although one of two things always happened; namely, either that the Circumlocution Office had nothing to say and said it, or that it had something to say which the honorable gentleman blundered one half and forgot the other; the Circumlocution Office was always voted immaculate by an accommodating majority.

Such a nursery of statesmen had the Department become in virtue of a long career of this nature, that several solemn statesmen had attained the reputation of being quite unearthly prodigies of business, solely from having practiced How not to do it, at the head of the Circumlocution Office. As to the minor priests and acolytes of that temple, the result of all this was that they stood divided into two classes, and down to the junior messenger, either believed in the Circumlocution Office as a heaven-born institution, that had an absolute right to do whatever it liked; or took refuge in total infidelity, and considered it a flagrant nuisance. . . .

When that admirable Department got into trouble, and was, by some infuriated Congressman, whom the smaller statesmen almost suspected of laboring under diabolic possession, attacked on the merits of no individual case, but as an institution wholly abominable and Bedlamite; then the honorable statesman who represented it in the House, would smite that member and cleave him asunder, with a statement of the quantity of business (for the prevention of business) done by the Circumlocution Office. Then would that honorable statesman hold in his hand a paper containing a few figures to which, with the permission of the House, he would entreat its attention. Then would the inferior statesmen exclaim, obeying orders, "Hear, Hear, Hear!" and "Read!" Then would the honorable statesman perceive, sir, from this little document, which he thought might carry conviction even to the perversest mind (Derisive laughter and cheering from the statesmen fry), that within the short compass of the last financial half-year, this much maligned Department (Cheers) had written and received fifteen thousand letters (Loud cheers), had made twenty-four thousand minutes (Louder cheers), and thirty-two thousand five hundred and seventeen memoranda (Vehement cheering). Nay, an ingenious gentleman connected with the Department, and himself a valuable public servant, had done him the favor to make a curious calculation of the amount of stationery consumed in it during the same period. It formed a part of this same short document; and he derived from it the remarkable fact that the sheets of paper it had devoted to the public service would pave the sidewalks on both sides of Pennsylvania Avenue from end to end, and leave nearly a quarter of a mile to spare. . . . Then, amidst a burst of official exultation, would the honorable statesman sit down, leaving the mutilated fragment of the Member on the field. No one, after that exemplary demolition of him, would have the hardihood to hint that the more the Circumlocution Office did, the less was done, and that the greatest blessing it could confer on an unhappy public would be to do nothing.

As the observant gentleman who wrote the Book of Ecclesiastes mentions, "That which hath been is that which shall be; and that which hath been done is that which shall be done: and there is no new thing under the sun."

8

---•◦—◦▸◦—◦•---

Maneuvers and Stratagems
of Older People

Every period of life presents its own special problems of interpersonal adjustment to the people passing through it. In old age a person encounters a new set of challenges and difficulties, and he meets them at a time of life when his mental ingenuity and physical strength are declining. Hence, old age has its own particular maneuvers and stratagems, and we shall consider a few of them in this chapter. These maneuvers and stratagems are important, for they determine whether the last decade of life is a peaceful Indian summer or a barren fall.

House Cleaning

House Cleaning is a vicious put-off stratagem executed by an elderly person who wishes to rid himself of the annoyance of a disabled spouse who no longer serves his interests and convenience. It is a stratagem which is increasing in frequency as a larger percentage of the population live into old age and develop the disabilities of senescence. Mrs. Finch was an excellent operator of this stratagem, and we shall dissect her brilliant tactics in detail.

175

Mrs. Finch was a sixty-five-year-old lady who had been married to her husband for forty-one years, and a good deal it was. Mr. Finch was a passive, anxious, hard-working certified public accountant whom Mrs. Finch dominated from the beginning of their marriage. To say that Mrs. Finch was in love with her husband when she married him would be to use the word loosely, for Mrs. Finch had a prior affection which preempted any true passion for Mr. Finch. Mrs. Finch's first, and enduring, love was herself. Raised by indulgent parents who let her have her way in everything, she was so much impressed with the value of herself that her enduring affections were turned inward. She was charming, well educated, socially graceful and good-looking. She dressed with éclat and she spoke with vivacity. Altogether, she was a good wife, except that she had no affection to give and required an obliging submissiveness from the people around her.

She chose her husband (and she chose him; he did not choose her) with skill. Mr. Finch met her needs well. He was passive and easily dominated and, at the same time, he was hard-working and a good money-maker. He came from a "nice family" and he was preeminently socially presentable. He balded early, which made him look older than he was and made her look younger than she was when they went out together in public. Their home was a showplace, their social life brilliant, their appearance in public charming, and their sex life dreary and barren. Mrs. Finch found sex an inconvenient, messy affair and obliged Mr. Finch only occasionally. She confidently knew that he was too shy and too afraid of her to seek warmer women elsewhere. She knew the maneuvers to whip him into line at the least sign of independence or rebellion. She was master of the rasping invective, the guilt-slinging slash, and the belittling body blow. If these time-tested weapons did not quickly reduce Mr. Finch to quivering and apologetic obedience, a hysterical temper tantrum annihilated him and brought him to her bedside with tearful contrition whenever he had complained mildly of the cost of their way of life or had demurred at one of her demands.

Mr. Finch had been excellently trained by a domineering, guilt-slinging mother, and his wife continued this work with equal skill.

All in all, their friends found them a model couple in society; they were envied for their affluence, and Mr. Finch blinked mildly behind his spectacles at dinner parties and made light talk while his wife shone as a social figure in their city. This marriage produced one child, a daughter who was dominated by Mrs. Finch until she fled into marriage with a dentist at the age of twenty-one. She made him a good wife, but she had many physical complaints which were largely emotional in origin and which usually were worse when she had contact with her mother. However, on the surface she was the Ideal Daughter to her Charming Mother and Fine Father.

So the Finches coasted pleasantly through life, and they dined out, they entertained and were entertained in return, they dressed well, they ate well, they looked well, and were, all in all, Very Happy. So this envied couple arrived into their sixties. Being a partner in his own public accounting firm, Mr. Finch continued to work as he entered his late sixties, when misfortune entered their home. For, even to so well adjusted a couple as the Finches, misery can come. One day a demon entered their lovely house and destroyed Mr. Finch.

The demon came one evening after dinner as Mr. Finch sat watching one of his wife's favorite television programs with her. The demon put a dreadful finger on a major artery of Mr. Finch's brain and Mr. Finch felt dizzy and confused. He became nauseated and had numbness in his left arm and leg. He tried to get up, but was too weak to rise. His wife glared at him in annoyance that he should spoil her enjoyment of her program; after all, it came only once a week. However, a closer look at Mr. Finch spread alarm even to the well-tempered bosom of Mrs. Finch, for Mr. Finch's mouth drooped at the left corner, the lines of his face on that side were flattened, and his cheek hung limp. He struggled

177

helplessly but could not move his left arm and leg. The demon had invaded their home and had left *Mrs.* Finch with a stroke.

Note that although Mr. Finch was paralyzed, it was Mrs. Finch whom the demon had struck. For suddenly Mr. Finch had ceased to be the useful, obliging, money-coining, socially presentable gentleman he had been for forty-one years. The demon had made him a Thing. He was helplessly chained in the prison of his own body. He could no longer mix cocktails, run errands, go to the office, pay bills and do all the other things he had done for Mrs. Finch for forty-one years. The cruel demon had bound him to a wheelchair and he had to be waited on and helped to eat. He had to be maneuvered to the toilet and he had to be carted to bed. Cruel, cruel demon who had so unpleasantly complicated the life of Mrs. Finch. Mrs. Finch thought about this injustice with quiet fury as she watched Mr. Finch during the first few weeks of his stroke. She felt immensely injured, very much put upon, and she suffered terribly.

It became clear after a couple of months that Mr. Finch would not recover. His doctor was a devoted man who liked Ed Finch and, of all their friends, understood a bit more of his life than the others. He cared for him with diligence and Ed Finch did not die. He came home from the hospital with a practical nurse, a bosomy fifty-one-year-old grandmother of working-class background who had gone into practical nursing when all her children had grown up and were married or in military service. She fussed over Mr. Finch, fed him, read the sports page of the newspaper to him (her favorite page, not his, but he appreciated the attention), and he was introduced to the unsolved mystery of how the local citizenry remained faithful to their major-league baseball team despite the fact that it lost continually. All in all, Ed Finch, in the hands of his doctor and the practical nurse, could have lived several years, quietly wheeled in the sunshine by his talkative nurse who found him "such a fine figure of a man, even at his age and in spite of his trouble, you know." His doctor, who was more a friend than a physician, visited him twice a week and always found his color looking better and "his spirits looking up." It would have made a quiet Indian summer to a life that had been passed in endless work at the office and a continual social treadmill.

However, this would be a cruel life for that excellent lady Mrs. Finch. For to her Mr. Finch was now a Thing, an inconvenient Thing and, above all, an expensive Thing. Moreover, the Finches did not have as much money as their friends might have calculated. The Good Life costs money, and Mrs. Finch had been entitled to the Good Life and she had had it. With Mr. Finch not working but costing so much a day instead, he was a loss on the marital books. Of course, with reasonable planning the finances would fit, but there would have to be cuts here and there. There would be no more Caribbean cruises in January, no more shopping trips to New York, and no more summers at Cape Cod. The cruel demon had done all this to her. Also, the demon had worked another ironic trick on the much mistreated Mrs. Finch. Mr. Finch had a load of life insurance, and the unpleasant fact was that he would have been worth a nice pile of money if he were completely a Thing—that is, dead—rather than only half a Thing—that is, an invalid.

Obviously, the situation called for a stratagem. And five months after the demon struck the cruel blow of Stroke, Mrs. Finch began her stratagem. She had never been at a loss for maneuvers and stratagems to get what she wanted all her life, and the muses who watch over the Beautiful and the Successful certainly would not desert her now when she needed them so much. The muses did not desert her. They delivered into her hands the House Cleaning stratagem, used by many people before her and destined to be used by legions more after her. Then the muses bound a silken scarf over Mrs. Finch's eyes so she could go to work and not see what she was doing. For the muses had arranged to help Mrs. Finch make Mr. Finch a complete Thing instead of only half a Thing.

The stratagem of House Cleaning took four months. First Mrs. Finch found she could not stand so crude and boorish a woman as the practical nurse. She was "perhaps a good woman in her own way," but her manners were "lower-class," her uniforms had wrinkles in the wrong places as they spread over her ample bosom, and she once committed the unpardonable sin of calling Mrs. Finch "dearie" while they were helping Mr. Finch into his wheelchair. Such a lower-class phenomenon could not be allowed to contaminate the lovely home of the Finches, and she was let go. Mr. Finch had a wet eye when Mrs. McCollum left (for that was the lowerclass phenomenon's name), but no one noted that, and Mrs. McCollum blew her nose on a large handkerchief and said she would telephone once every few days to see how Mr. Finch was getting along. However, Mrs. Finch received these calls with such efficient, brief formality that they soon stopped. Mrs. McCollum's duties devolved upon Mary Beth, the full-time maid. Besides cooking, cleaning the house and helping Mrs. Finch to get ready to go out, Mary Beth was to look after Mr. Finch. So Mr. Finch sat alone most of the time in a little back room and stared out the window into the neighbors' yard while Mary Beth took care of all the other things Mrs. Finch required of her. As the weeks went by, Mr. Finch began to fail. He ate poorly, he slept poorly, he soiled himself with urine once in a while, and his face became haggard. Obviously, he was doing poorly.

Mrs. Finch, of course, knew just what the trouble was. He was being exhausted by too much visiting. Hence, she told the old friends who came three or four times a week to visit Mr. Finch that he needed "more rest" and he "wasn't up to all this visiting," and the visitors ceased to come. The doctor protested strongly that Mr. Finch needed the visitors, as he had protested that Mr. Finch needed Mrs. McCollum, but Mrs. Finch replied with supreme self-confidence that she "had been married to Ed Finch for forty-one years and knew his moods better than anyone." After all, the doctor hadn't been married to Ed Finch for forty-one years, and she persisted in her statements until she had her way. So Ed Finch sat in isolation day in and day out looking at the neighbors' backyard. Winter came, and the neighbors went to spend two months with their married daughter in Texas, and then there was not much to see in the neighbors' backyard.

Ed Finch grew silent. He rarely talked. Mrs. Finch scolded him about his "sullen attitude." Livid annoyance sat in her face that she should be laden with such a burden, and her annoyance seeped out in the impatient word, the brusque gesture, and the way she pressed her lips together when she was with him. Ed Finch died within himself, but he went on living. The stratagem of House Cleaning was nearing its end. One morning when Mrs. Finch was at a friend's house and Mary Beth was running the washing machine in the basement, Ed Finch slowly and painfully wheeled himself into the hall and then into a small library which they had made years ago by closing a screened porch and lining it with walnut-paneled bookshelves. Somehow or other, he pulled himself up to the fifth tier of books, and a cascade of books tumbled down over him as he pawed for something behind the books. He clutched it, but in doing so, he lost his balance and fell to the floor. Mary Beth in the basement heard the noise and started upstairs. When she was halfway up the stairs she heard a pistol shot. The stratagem of House Cleaning was over.

Mrs. Finch's friends were solicitous for her after the funeral. She had suffered so much with Mr. Finch during his last illness.

The Turveydrop Stratagem

The Turveydrop stratagem, which might be subtitled "How to Be Supported by Your Children While Proclaiming That You Are Doing Them a Favor," is a common stratagem executed by elderly people who live with their children. Though it masquerades as a come-on tactic, it is a put-off stratagem which creates dissension in the home and drives family members apart from one another. It sometimes is an economic necessity for an elderly person to live with an adult son or daughter. If the elderly person and the adult child frankly admit to themselves and to each other that the monthly Social Security check does not enable the elderly person to live separately, they often can live together in reasonable harmony. However, if the elderly person feels shame and embarrassment about having to live with an adult child, he may begin to evolve a Turveydrop stratagem, in which he rationalizes that moving in with his adult child is a magnificent favor he is rendering him. He begins to carry out one of the stratagems we shall discuss in this section, and he demands the gratitude and praise of his children for the alleged benefits he is conferring on them. This type of stratagem is labeled a Turveydrop stratagem after one of its most accomplished practitioners, Mr. Turveydrop of Dickens' novel *Bleak House,* who skillfully inflicted himself on his son and daughter-in-law and talked unceasingly of the mythical benefits he claimed to be lavishing on them by living with them.

We shall consider a few of the ways the Turveydrop stratagem may be executed.

I'm Going to Help You Rear Your Children

In this variety of the Turveydrop stratagem the elderly parent moves in with the ostensible purpose of directing her adult son or daughter in rearing the children. The older person presents excellent credentials for this work; she reared either the wife or the husband, and, after all, the other one of the marital couple chose the product of her child-rearing for a spouse. Hence, both of them stand as witnesses to the older person's skill in rearing children. Any defects apparent in the product of this child-rearing are tactfully ignored.

An old law of physics states that two finite objects cannot occupy the same space at the same time. Similarly, two females cannot rear the same child at the same time, and this is especially true when the rival mothers are mother-in-law and daughter-in-law. The mother-in-law's theme is: "I reared your husband and look how well he turned out, so kindly move aside and let me perform an equal service for your child." The daughter-in-law's theme is: "My husband turned out well in spite of the way you reared him, and I intend to rear my son as I see fit." The husband's theme becomes: "I wish they'd raise the monthly Social Security payments so Mom could move out of here and we'd have some peace once more." The children's theme becomes Divide and Rule (see Chapter 4 for the diabolical ways enterprising children play adults off against each other in this stratagem). Various complex maneuvers and stratagems dominate every aspect of family life.

The dinner table becomes a testing ground where the competing mothers use coaxing, threats and bribes to get the child to eat his vegetables. The mother-in-law and daughter-in-law vie to outdo each other in the maneuver Look How I Can Get Him to Eat After You Failed. Bribes tumble forth from both competitors as the artful child plays them off against each other and waits for the highest bid to come through. When the highest bid comes, the child knocks down the item, eats his vegetables and walks off with the payment, which may be privileges, gifts, money or merely the joy of seeing adults in abject submission to him.

Bedtime is another excellent occasion for the child to pit his rival mothers against each other. By skillfully exploiting their anxiousness to be his favorite, he usually can wheedle an extra hour of television time out of the situation. As one mother tries to get him into bed, the other says, "Why, he's not tired and won't be able to sleep yet; so he can watch television a little longer." The defeated mother fumes inwardly as the artful child cuddles in the lap of her competitor. Not to be outdone, the defeated mother the next night makes even greater concessions to win over the child, and she feels sweet revenge as the child now cuddles with her. Soon the child is watching whatever television programs he wants until whatever hour he chooses.

In the end, neither mother rears the child. He rears himself with both mothers as his obliging servants. Hence the stratagem I'm Going to Help You Rear Your Child usually ends up as Neither One of Us Will Rear the Child.

I'm Going to Redeem You

In this variety of the Turveydrop stratagem the older person defines moving in with his children as a campaign to secure their religious redemption by "bringing religion into the home." The older person proclaims that the younger generation is going to perdition because of its lack of firm religious training, but that this religious vitality is yet preserved in the vessels of the older generation for the salvation of the young. The elderly Protestant carts in his Bible, the aging Catholic hauls in rosaries and crucifixes, and the elderly Jew drags in prayer shawls or a collection of dishes, pots and pans for the installation of a kosher kitchen or at least a kosher corner in the kitchen. The adult children cringe as they witness this invasion, for few things are harder to fight than religious redemption promoted by an elderly strategist engaged in I'm Going to Redeem You.

A skillful opening move often is to institute saying grace at meals. At first the prayers are short and perfunctory, but in time they grow longer. Then saying grace is foisted on others by gentle nudges such as "Stanton, will you say grace today?" or "Julia, will you ask the blessing?" The ravenous children are firmly corrected if they grab the bread before grace is said, and adults get cold stares if they jump the gun. Once established, grace is an opening wedge to jam in other religious practices, by including prayers in the grace such as "and may the whole family pray together in church tomorrow" or "may this Christmas truly be blessed as a religious season and not as a cocktail party time. . . ."

The next step is to drag everybody, willing or unwilling, rebellious or subdued, to church. As everyone is corralled on Sunday morning, the adults mutter, "I don't remember that we went to church much when I was a kid. When did Mom get so all-fired religious?" and "You never told me your mother was such a nut on going to church." The adult children often rebel; Father grabs his golf clubs, Mother seizes her garden tools, and they elude the oldster's grasp. However, the resourceful strategist, determined to redeem at least part of the family and seizing that part which is most defenseless, corners the children, gets them dressed in tight-fitting Sunday clothes and ostentatiously carts them off to services as souls redeemed in spite of the sloth of their parents. "If I weren't here they'd all be raised heathens" ennobles the older person's presence in the home as a crusader who is going to save the family in spite of themselves.

Jewish families have their own special trials with I'm Going to Redeem You strategists. Mothers and fathers quake as they see the candles come out on Friday nights or hear Grandfather's loud Hebraic muttering descending from an upstairs bedroom where some very audible praying is going on with the door wide open. Grandma barricades the kitchen with kosher dishes, pots and pans arrayed in meticulous confusion which only she can keep track of. Two women in one kitchen is bad enough, but when one is manipulating a kosher kitchen and the other is serving TV dinners, the result is $E = MC^2$.

The older person becomes increasingly religious as he bashes the family down with his superior devoutness. People who rarely went to church in their forties struggle to services in their sixties even when racked by arthritis and wheezing coughs. Old Catholics who attended mass once a month in their youth find they cannot carry on without it daily after they move in with their children and begin the stratagem of I'm Going to Redeem You. Old Jews who were never seen near a synagogue in their youth except on Yom Kippur and Rosh Hashana suddenly find they cannot live without evening prayers or the clatter of kosher dishware.

The young children, as well as their parents, who live in an I'm Going to Redeem You household end up either religious or rebellious, usually the latter. The older person wins no matter what happens. He either leads the family triumphantly into religiosity (and thus in payment for a little bread from them in this world provides handsomely for them in the next), or he can parade his superior sanctity in front of the cowed, guilt-ridden family. All in all, this is a good stratagem for the old person to execute; an alliance with the Deity gives the strategist a powerful ally, and combating the two of them is difficult.

I'm Going to Reform You

In this stratagem the older person moves in with the family with the ostensible mission of reforming their way of life. Alcohol is a favorite point of first attack. The evening cocktail of the adult children elicits a pained frown and the observation that "Your dear departed father never drank that stuff." As the young adult couple go out the door to a party, an anxious inquiry floats after them, "Will alcohol be served there?" in a tone that says, "What kind of sin will go on tonight?" The next morning a red-eyed old lady observes, "I couldn't go to sleep until I heard you come in, what with worrying about Tom driving home after a party like that. You know, fifty percent of all fatal accidents occur after drinking alcohol." A smashed fender or a dented car door after a party open a breach into which the strategist leaps with undisguised triumph.

Extravagance with money is another point at which the I'm Going to Reform You strategist attacks. "Your father and I never squandered money on things like that. We knew we had four children to put through college." "Young people nowadays need so many things to get along. I wonder how they can afford it and where it all will end." "In my day mothers never worked out of the home. We lived within our means so we could stay home and rear our children." The phrase "living beyond their means" becomes a bludgeon with which children are bloodied daily as the old person carries out a good stratagem of I'm Going to Reform You.

The reformer preaches the simple joys of life, as opposed to the frivolous excitements of "modern young people." "Your daddy and I stayed at home and loved our little home. We didn't have to be running to country clubs, bowling alleys, bridge parties and all these other places all the time." Thus, by constant preaching of sobriety, thrift and contentment with simple things, the strategist elevates living with his children to a self-sacrificing crusade against whiskey, insolvency and social delinquency.

I'm Going to Support You

This is another stratagem in the armamentarium of the Turveydrop strategist. It may appear strange that a parent who is moving into his child's home because he cannot support himself should execute a stratagem titled I'm Going to Support You, but a skillful strategist can work this one and even convince people of it. It all hinges on the thesis I'm Going to Show You How to Save So Much Money That I'll Solve All Your Financial Problems for You. The strategist assaults the young couple with a bewildering array of penny-saving devices which drive them to distraction. He or she preaches the economy of canned goods as opposed to frozen foods, of personally mowing the grass instead of paying the teenager next door to do it, of giving up smoking, of abandoning the evening cocktail, and of doing all home repairing and painting yourself instead of being robbed by "those modern bandits, the union plumbers and painters."

These money-saving suggestions spread into so many areas of family activities that everybody stumbles over them at every step. If the young couple ignores them, the words "extravagance" and "unpaid bills" are bandied about as the oldster courageously attempts to stave off insolvency despite "no cooperation from anybody else in the house." Thus, the strategist either corners his children into annoying minor economies or concludes with "Well, I could have saved them a mint of money, but I got no cooperation."

The obvious solution to all kinds of Turveydrop stratagems is for the elderly person to face the fact that living with his children is the only economically practical thing to do and to drop the stratagems with which he is attempting to camouflage this fact. However, the old person's shame and embarrassment about his dependency make this a difficult step for him to take. Nevertheless, if the person and his children become articulately aware of existence of the Turveydrop stratagem in their home, they often can rid themselves of it, since many of these people have basically sound personalities and have been pushed into Turveydrop stratagems by the difficulties of adjusting to an embarrassing, but very common, human predicament.

Grandma in Wonderland

The term Grandma in Wonderland covers a wide spectrum of maneuvers and stratagems employed by elderly people in dealing with a common dilemma of old age, the slow deterioration of their intellectual capacities. Modern medicine has increased the life-span until the majority of people live into their late sixties, their seventies or their eighties. In advanced age a slow, progressive dulling of intellectual capacities frequently occurs owing to narrowing of blood vessels of the brain and degeneration of brain cells. The person has impairment of memory, especially memory of recent events. His orientation in time and place becomes blurred and his judgment weakens. Skills and knowledge slip from him, and he gropes his way into the senile confusion of old age. This process does not happen to all old people, but it happens to a large number of them. When the poet Browning wrote, "Grow old along with me, the best is yet to be/The last of life for which the first was made," he was taking a very optimistic view of threescore and ten.

In coping with this process the elderly person faces a dilemma unlike any he has previously encountered. Fortunately the gentler Fates who preside over old age give him a little help in finding ways to dull the pain and assuage the alarm caused by the slow deterioration of his mind. First of all, they arrange that his memory loss shall start with the most recent things in his life and leave the older things more intact. Thus, the failing old person may not be able to remember the events of the past few days, or of recent months and years, but he can remember the details of weddings, births and child-rearing events that happened twenty years or more ago. In this way the Fates lead him away from the painful present, blot it out, move back the calendar, and gently lead him into the wonderland of the past, and they give the past the vivid urgency of the present.

Next, the Fates take away much of the passion and vigor which propelled the person onward during his lifetime. The goading prods of sexual passion, the restless lure of money, the aching appetites of the body, and the competitive race for prestige and privilege recede. The elderly person now is free to wander in peace in the old past of former years, in the wonderland to which failing memory of recent events has led him.

The Fates have a third precious gift for the old person whom they lead into wonderland. They disguise death so that the old person forgets its imminence and terror as he wanders in the wonderland of lost years. When the Gray Angel comes at last, he gently takes the old person by the hand, and the elderly person does not know with whom he is walking or where. Those who dread senility see only its hard features and are unaware of its kinder aspects. After all, there is something to be said for the Puzzled Angel who robs a man of his awareness before the terror of death affronts him.

As Grandma enters wonderland she begins to employ various tactics to adjust to her new surroundings. She fills up her memory gaps with fictions of many kinds. I recall a seventy-eight-year-old lady from whom the Puzzled Angel took all memory of the last seventy years of her life, and into this gap Grandma fabricated a wonderland of childhood, mixing adventures that never occurred with many events that did occur. She laughed, scolded and rambled through the endless experiences of her childhood in Sweden, even losing the stumbling English she had learned in America and returning to the gabbling Swedish she had spoken in her childhood. She cast off the tight shoes of a foreign tongue and put on the easy slippers of her native language. She gave everyone new roles. Her adult children became her long-dead brothers and sisters, and she chattered at them and giggled over childhood jokes. She scolded them over arguments that occurred seventy years before. She transformed her room in the nursing home into the cottage where she was raised, and by the magic stratagem of Grandma in Wonderland the nurses and attendants became neighbors and visiting friends. When the Gray Angel paid his call one Thursday afternoon she did not recognize him and mistook him for a gentler visitor; he led her away without protest and without terror. After all, what child of eight expects the Gray Angel or would know him if he appeared?

Sometimes the old person in wonderland builds castles; he wanders in their imposing corridors, looks forth from their gargoyled ramparts onto his vast estates and gives orders to the hordes of obliging subjects who obey him. I recall an old man who sat day in and day out on the porch of his small home staring at the quiet, tree-lined street in front of him. Neighbors who passed looked pityingly at poor old Mr. Levine, who just sat there all day long. But had they known the wonderland of Mr. Levine, they might have envied him instead. For the Puzzled Angel had touched the memory of Mr. Levine and had taken from him remembrance of the small dry-cleaning shop he had run for forty years. The Puzzled Angel took away the memory of the steaming presses on hot summer days, the long hours to catch the customers on their way to work or on their way home at night, the sniping complaints about the spots that wouldn't come out and the colors that wouldn't stay in, the dull terror of the months when business was bad and the frantic rushing of the months when business was good. What did the Puzzled Angel give Mr. Levine in exchange for forty years in a cramped shop? The Puzzled Angel was lavish with Mr. Levine. She gave him a factory where all sorts of wonderful things were made by good employees for grateful customers, and Mr. Levine babbled about "the plant" and "the big orders we got today" and "the big shipments we will make tomorrow" and "the big money we're making here." When people tried to bother him with the present and his annoyed or wet-eyed children tried to orient him to the events of the day, he would push them aside; he thought they were his cousins and his brothers, and he told them he didn't have time for all this sort of thing but "must be off to the office." And everyone pitied poor old Mr. Levine and commented on "how bad he had gone downhill," but Mr. Levine's friend the Puzzled Angel smiled at them and pitied them in return.

I recall a senile, rambling gentleman of eighty-four who came from a nursing home to the hospital to have a lobe of his prostate cut out. We residents and interns—all of us embroiled with our endless work, our girlfriends or our wives, and our children crying at midnight or sniffling with colds at breakfast—regarded the old gentleman as a sort of Thing whom our professional ethics required us to patch up to go on living when life no longer meant anything. One morning on the ward I saw Mr. Donaldson laughing to himself and leering about. When I asked him what was so pleasant, he motioned to me to come close to him, and he confided in an excited whisper that the little student nurse bending over a bed down the ward was "a mighty good piece of ass" (as she may well have been), and he chuckled as he told me how he had taken her to bed the night before and "what a dish she was." Then he winked at me and settled back in bed. Also, I fear I once caught Mr. Donaldson masturbating under the sheets while he grinned at a handsome nurse. The other interns in time noted Old Donaldson's fanciful preoccupations with our pretty nurses and the ways he concocted love affairs with them while never leaving his bed and with a urinary bladder tube draining from him into a large glass jug under the bed. I suppose the Puzzled Angel cheated a little in giving Old Donaldson some illicit pleasures that angels really are not supposed to arrange. Perhaps the Puzzled Angel received a gentle reproof from her Celestial Superiors for being so indulgent with him. As we interns and residents struggled with our long working hours, our crabbing superiors and our anxieties when our girlfriends had late monthly periods, we joked about Old Donaldson's "romances." However, the Puzzled Angel probably smiled pityingly at us as she fussed over her child and took care of him. For Old Donaldson had passionate rendezvous with the choicest nurses and never had to worry about pregnancies or competition from the chief resident. He had the delights of the marital bed without the hair curlers and irritable words at the breakfast table. He had the fun of sex without the midnight howling of fretful babies and the coughing of croupy children. The Puzzled Angel has an endless store of gifts for her charges, and she is generous in distributing them.

Of course, it must be admitted that the Puzzled Angel *is* puzzled, and she is very busy since she has so many people to take care of these days. Terror and confusion sometimes assail her children, and they may become peevish, querulous or violent. However, the Puzzled Angel usually comes running, her robes disarrayed, and she shoves a clutch of maneuvers and stratagems at her upset child. Soon he is soothed and wandering in wonderland again.

The Dying Tigress

One of the first psychiatric patients I saw was an elderly lady who was presented to the medical students at grand rounds when I was in medical school. She was a determined old lady in her seventies who glared at us furiously. She looked imperiously at the resident physician who presented her case, as a medieval baroness would have looked at a lackey whom she was about to order to the courtyard to receive fifty lashes. The professor asked her a few questions and she answered with brief severity. Then she was escorted out in her wheelchair by a waiting nurse and was taken back to her room.

The professor was a courtly, erudite German who had fled the horrors of Nazi Europe to come to teach in America. He combined high clinical acumen with a touch of poetry. "This woman," he began, "is a dying tigress," and he went on to talk about her case. All her life she was a domineering woman who ruled her husband, her children and her carefully selected friends with an iron hand. Obedience merited reward and resistance aroused a slashing attack. After an attack or two, a victim rarely resisted her again. The Tigress strode majestic and supreme in her grove, and a handsome Tigress she was—a tall, beautiful woman, well dressed and well groomed. She knew how to walk well, and she talked charmingly, and when the Tigress was pleased she was gracious and fascinating.

However, old age had dealt harshly with our Tigress. Her brilliant white teeth were replaced with dentures, her marble skin became sprinkled with the brown spots of age, her stately walk became stooped, her straight nose curved down over her mouth, and her full cheeks sank inward. Her graceful fingers were studded with the knots of arthritis and her once full figure was wilted. Her dresses hung loose on her bony body, and her glance was dull behind bifocals. Her memory for facts, faces and names was less acute. She knew what was happening to her and she was terrified and furious.

Time was dealing cruelly with our imperious Tigress, and as if in payment for her past brutal domination of others, the Puzzled Angel of senile oblivion did not come to take away the memory of her past glory in contrast with her present dreariness and to fill her mind with a fairy wonderland of pleasant fictions. The Tigress' raging will to dominate still burned in her and she was determined still to stride in stateliness when she could only ride in a wheelchair. She was desperate and defiant, and she lashed out in futile maneuvers and stratagems to clutch the control which was rapidly leaving her.

Since then I have seen many Dying Tigresses, and Dying Tigers too—achieving, commanding people, struggling to maintain domination over others while watching it slip away from them. The old maneuvers and stratagems no longer work; the hostility and guilt-slinging fail to corral their children into docile obedience, and long-used temper tantrums with sobbing reproaches of ingratitude are looked on as sickness rather than commands. The Dying Tigresses and Tigers threaten suicide as the final act to which their disobedient children have driven them; they menace them with the guilt of having killed a parent, but these threats no longer stampede the people around them. The decline of their physical and mental agility robs them of the skill they once had in maneuvers and stratagems, and commands that once seemed compelling now seem ridiculous. Moreover, the people who formerly were dominated know that disability is drawing the teeth of the Tigresses and Tigers and clipping their claws and that death waits close behind. The Tigresses and Tigers are losing their terror for people. But still the Dying Tigress or Dying Tiger puts up a final lashing battle and may spread ruin about him; sometimes he destroys much of the work of a lifetime in the thrashings of his final agony. The Dying Tigress is a put-off stratagem which splits the Tigress off from family members and often disrupts other family relationships.

I recall a seventy-one-year-old woman who for eighteen years had run a family business after the death of her husband. Though she had always been a domineering, temper-tantrumish person who bullied her husband and children, she had become more rasping as she tasted the power and prestige of running her husband's business. At first she had said she would only fill her husband's place until her two sons graduated from college and entered the business. But when her sons entered the business, she began a complex series of maneuvers and stratagems to keep them dominated and to remain in control. She put her sons behind imposing desks but gave them trivial responsibilities while she ran the business with the help of two older employees who had held subordinate positions under her husband. Neither of these men was capable of assuming the responsibilities over other employees which she gave them. However, they served her purposes well, even though they served the interests of the business poorly. These men floundered in their work, were frightened by their responsibilities and clung to the Tigress for all decisions that had to be made. They ran to her with both large and small problems, and through them she controlled the business and excluded her sons. She remained dominant and imperious, both in the business and at home.

When her sons attempted to point out that the business was declining, that many decisions were being delayed until they were meaningless, that outdated systems were being used while their competitors were using modern methods, and that the men she was using were incompetent, the Tigress used in the business the same maneuvers of domination she used at home. She accused her sons of ingratitude for all her work to hold the business together after their father died, she bewailed her years of "backbreaking work in this business, which has taken years off my life," and she ranted about how she and her husband had worked night and day building up the business when her sons were children; this last diatribe was untrue, for she had nothing to do with the business until her husband died.

Her favorite technique for crushing her sons was to put in long hours at the business and then to deride her sons for the lesser time they spent in it. By these long hours in the business she felt she staked out a claim to dominate it. She arrived at seven in the morning and often stayed until eight at night, and her lunch and dinner were sent in from a neighboring café. The work she did was a meaningless sequence of trivial tasks that should have been done by secretaries and clerks, and the crucial work of the business was not done at all. However, when her sons objected to any of her decisions in the business, she retorted, "What does a nine-to-five employee who spends Saturdays on a golf course know about this business? I've been here from seven to eight, day in and day out since your father died, and he and I worked our fingers to the bone to start this business. Now you want to tell me how to run it. All you and your brother want is to take money out of this business. You're living well enough on it, aren't you? When you put in the hours I put in, you'll have the right to tell me how to run this business, but not until then." Attempts to point out that her time was spent doing work her incompetent assistants should have been doing or that any clerk could do only precipitated raging temper tantrums. Her sons, both of whom were well trained and capable, retreated before the slashing guilt-slinging and angry tirades of the Tigress. For twelve years they watched the business deteriorate as the Tigress imperiously ran it, enjoying immensely the role of an executive and the reputation of a wealthy businesswoman.

Then, early one March morning, her older son got a telephone call from his mother's maid. "Mrs. Rosen can't move her legs. She can't get out of bed, and she's awful upset." The son went at once to his mother's home, where he found her terrified and furious, paralyzed from the waist down. The family internist arrived forty-five minutes later, and that morning Mrs. Rosen entered the hospital. "I'll get over this in a few days and be back down at the office," she promised. She had a telephone installed in her room and attempted to run the business from her hospital bed, with office girls running to and fro with messages. She became more frightened and desperate each week as her legs refused to regain their strength and she lost control over bowel and urine functions. As she saw her strength leaving her and her domination of both her family and the business slipping from her, her shrieking temper tantrums became so unruly that her doctor threatened to transfer her to the psychiatric ward because other patients on the floor and their relatives complained about the noise. Under this threat she became quiet for two days, but then her howling fury began again, and, under pressure from the hospital administrators, she was transferred to the psychiatric division of the hospital where I watched her decline while her internist struggled with her physical problems.

As the weeks went by and word spread in business circles that Mrs. Rosen was paralyzed and "a little out of her mind," both the employees and the people with whom the firm did business began to turn to her sons for decisions and business dealings. Thus, the sons gradually took over the business, and in six months they were running it completely. Under their management it in time became financially sound again.

Furious with her body which wouldn't obey her and with the loss of control over her family and the business, Mrs. Rosen shrieked at home for four more years, an imperious Tigress whom no one feared or obeyed. Her dominion was restricted to her bedroom where she raged at her servants and practical nurses and sobbed to them how her family had mistreated her and deserted her after her "lifetime of working and slaving for them." When her sons and their families came to visit her, she flailed them with accusations of ingratitude and shrieked that her sons were reducing them all to poverty by ruining the business. Her sons squirmed silently in their chairs for a while and then went away with her howling accusations of ingratitude and incompetence following them down the stairs. After four years of this torture, the Tigress died. She died in her sleep of a heart attack. Death came quietly and gently to close a turbulent, furious life. Her maneuvers and stratagems were over.

9

Stratagems by Which
People Become Things

In this chapter we shall discuss the stratagems by which a person turns himself into a Thing. By death a person ceases to be involved in interpersonal relationships and he becomes a Thing which his fellowmen bury in the ground. The act by which a person turns himself into a Thing is called suicide.

Psychiatric theory holds that in the vast majority of cases the person who commits suicide is motivated by unconscious feelings whose nature he does not understand and that these unconscious emotional forces are the product of past and present unhealthy interpersonal relationships. In this sense, suicide is an interpersonal act; it is a response to painful emotional turmoil generated by stresses between people. However, by this act the person withdraws himself from the world of interpersonal living and enters the vast universe of inanimate Things.

Suicide is the ultimate in put-off stratagems, and it is caused by the most powerful put-off forces which can exist in man. In murdering himself, a man inflicts the maximum hostility that a person can express on a living creature, and by becoming a Thing, he forever leaves the world of interpersonal relationships.

Suicide is the most common form of death a psychiatrist encounters in his practice, and it is far more common than the general public realizes or than official statistics indicate. Hence, it merits our attention as we survey the maneuvers and stratagems which people use in confronting the dilemmas of life. Although the official statistics show that slightly more than twenty thousand suicides occur in the United States each year, all students of suicide agree that the total is at least two to three times that high, and some authorities feel it may be even higher. A large number of suicides are recorded as natural deaths and accidents. Kindly family doctors and sympathetic coroners are pressed to spare the feelings of grieving families, and often they record falls from high windows and overdosages with sedatives as accidental deaths. Many deaths in midnight automobile crashes in which a solo driver smashes into a tree or a bridge abutment are suicidal rather than accidental. Officially, suicide is the eleventh most common cause of death in America, but if all suicides were actually counted as such, it would be at least ninth in rank. Suicide is fifth in the causes of death of physicians, and it is slightly more common among psychiatrists than in the general medical profession. Suicide ranks fourth as the cause of death in adolescents between the ages of fifteen and nineteen. Only one out of every ten to twenty serious suicidal attempts is successful. Hence, about two million persons living in America today at some time in their lives made a serious suicidal attempt.

To her victim Suicide seems to say, "Leave all the pain of living and enter my domain where neither the long agony of pain nor the brief fit of pleasure pursue you. Abandon the world of people and enter the world of Things, my eternal, calm, painless realm." Then Suicide speaks more pressingly as she sees her listener waver. "It is not a matter of whether or not you will come to me. It is only a matter of when you will come. All men are dying, though at slightly different rates of speed, and every minute brings you closer to me. You are only taking into your own hands what natural forces will soon do to you anyway. But they come slowly and rack you with pain, disease and the final slow agony. They let you suffer for years or decades before they complete their tardy job. I offer you now the peace of the world of Things."

We shall now consider in detail two stratagems of suicide. There are many more, but we shall restrict our attention to these two.

Garbage Like Me

Suicide sometimes follows decades of maneuvers and stratagems which fill the person with feelings of guilt and worthlessness. Stratagems like Sledge Hammer, Torture Rack, That Awful Woman, Queen Bee, You Can Never Repay Me and the Dying Tigress, which are discussed in earlier chapters, leave a person with profound feelings of guilt and unworthiness. In most instances, a combination of both past and present stratagems draws the person to suicide.

I recall a twenty-year-old girl whose mother had carried out a hard, cruel stratagem of You Can Never Repay Me all the girl's life. The mother was a rasping woman who used martyrdom and guilt-slinging to dominate the entire family, and the girl had been subjected to the endless grinding of You Can Never Repay Me all her life. In the girl's childhood her mother told her repeatedly how she had suffered agony in childbirth to give the girl the precious gift of life and how she had almost died in the process. The mother complained chronically of excruciating back pain which she said had begun when the girl was born. She proclaimed that she had worked from sunup to sundown racked with pain all the girl's life in order to rear her and that she had deprived herself of necessities to give the girl luxuries. In reality, her delivery of the girl had been normal, and no doctor had ever found a physical cause for her back pain, and their middle-class life had contained no more work than the lives of their neighbors. However, through this lifelong stratagem of I Suffered So Much to Rear You That You Can Never

Repay Me, the mother dominated the girl ruthlessly and made an obedient automaton out of her. She ruled her by flooding her with guilt and feelings of obligation.

In the process the mother left her daughter with profound feelings of Garbage Like Me. The girl felt worthless, inadequate and inferior, and she felt that she carried a contagion of misery with her which she inflicted on other people. Her mother's daily harangues represented reality to her.

When the girl was twenty she took a job as secretary in a large company. Her boss was an irritable man who was under chronic pressure from his boss, who was grinding him to the wall in a vicious stratagem of May the Best Man Win. Under other circumstances he might have been a reasonable employer, but under the daily pressures of the man who was pushing him out of the company with May the Best Man Win, he was critical and nasty in the office, and the girl received the full brunt of his irritability. This was her first job and her first major independent venture outside the home. Unfortunately, she encountered in it the same kind of deprecation that she had always had from her mother. Her worst fears of inadequacy and worthlessness seemed confirmed. At home, at work, everywhere, it seemed, she met the deprecation and hostility which could only mean that all the world treated her as she deserved to be treated, as Garbage Like Me.

One Friday afternoon she left her desk to go to the ladies' room in the tall office building in which she worked. Minutes later hundreds of heads poked out of the building windows to see what had brought the screaming sirens of ambulances and police patrol cars to the street below. A crowd was gathered around a splotch of yellow cloth with a shattered body in it. The stratagem of You Can Never Repay Me had come to an end. She had repaid in full.

Her death shows how the stratagems of life weave into each other in social relationships. She was, to a certain extent, a victim of the stratagem May the Best Man Win, which was being executed in the executive suite of the company for which she worked, in addition to the stratagem You Can Never Repay Me, which had been carried out in her home.

Miscalculated Risk

In some instances suicide is an accident by a person who uses threats of suicide and suicidal gestures as whips to manipulate his family. In some of these cases the empty nature of the suicidal gesture is obvious. I recall a young married woman who, after a spat with her husband, called him into the dining room where she stood in a melodramatic pose with a can opener pointed at her throat. Her husband was terrified and she won the day; he promised not to oppose her wishes further on the subject about which they had been arguing. It was a brief maneuver that gained her point. A similar maneuver is to swallow eight aspirin tablets and then to call the stampeded marital partner to the bedside for a final reconciliation before the demise. In similar maneuvers, husbands brandish empty pistols with loud cries of "I'm going to end it all," and frustrated adolescents rush into bathrooms and lock the door or run out the front door ostensibly headed for the superhighway. A few light nicks on the wrists with a razor sometimes corral an adolescent's resistant parents or a married person's recalcitrant spouse into docile obedience. Such maneuvers may happen once or twice in a lifetime, or they may be frequent methods by which the maneuverer manipulates his family. Sometimes an unwilling young man or lady is stampeded into marriage by "If we're not going to get married, I'd sooner die," followed by the ingestion of four or five sleeping pills or by a rush to the bathroom for razor blades. This is an ominous way to begin a marriage.

However, there is a broad no-man's-land between the suicidal gesture which is used to dominate people and the suicidal attempt which is an effort to terminate life. An old psychiatric axiom states that the person who pretends to have a psychiatric illness often ends up psychiatrically ill and that the person who uses suicide as a maneuver to control people has a much higher chance of eventually dying by suicide than persons in the general population. The emotional turmoil which led the person to use suicidal threats in dealing with people around him also causes a severe emotional illness years or decades later which ends in suicide. However, in some cases a suicidal gesture causes death by a Miscalculated Risk; the person accidentally misses his goal and kills himself by error.

Francine was the victim of a Miscalculated Risk. She was the forty-two-year-old wife of a dentist, and for several years she had dominated her husband, her three children, her parents and her in-laws by a skillfully executed stratagem of Torture Rack. She complained of many obscure, excruciating pains, and she ruled her family from the bed of an invalid. She saw doctors in various medical centers and she had many diagnostic work-ups. Each diagnostic procedure was followed by painful "side reactions." She shopped from doctor to doctor and from clinic to clinic. Many physicians suggested that her difficulties were emotional in nature, but after each suggestion of this sort she rejected her doctor and searched for a new one. Finally, after years of dominating her bedraggled family by Torture Rack, she was cornered by her relatives into psychiatric consultation. On the surface she accepted it; "I'll do anything to get well." However, she resisted each step of psychiatric treatment and clung tightly to the stratagem by which she ruled her family.

Then a subtle change began. She seemed to accept psychiatric treatment; she talked spontaneously in her interviews and appeared to be making progress. However, her progress was apparent rather than real. Within a few months it was clear that she merely had shifted her symptoms and tactics in a continuing stratagem of Torture Rack. Instead of physical pains (which now largely disappeared), she used dramatic agitation, sobbing depressiveness and threats of suicide to control her family. She had merely changed her symptoms in Torture Rack from physical ones to psychiatric ones, and the stratagem went on as before. Now her most potent weapons were suicidal threats and gestures which stampeded her relatives into doing whatever she wanted and made her home a nightmare. Repeated psychiatric hospitalizations for suicidal gestures, most of which were harmless, gave only brief relief to her family. Psychiatric treatment ground into a stalemate; it had merely become transformed into Psychiatric Torture Rack, which seemed destined to become a chronic pattern of family life that would last for decades.

Then one wet spring morning Francine took a fatal Miscalculated Risk. Her husband had been at his office for an hour when he received a call from Francine saying that since she couldn't prevail in a decision regarding their fifteen-year-old daughter, she knew she must be a "bad mother" and it would be better for all of them if she were dead. She said she had locked herself in her bedroom and was going to take some pills. She hung up the telephone. Her terrified husband left his office and started for home. Then Francine took two bottles of antidepressant pills which she had received from different doctors many months before and put them by her bedside with a glass of water. She unlocked her bedroom door, emptied each bottle of pills into the palm of her hand, put the pills in her mouth and washed them down with water. She then lay back on the pillows to await her husband's return.

But Francine had miscalculated badly. She thought that antidepressant pills, as opposed to sedatives, would not cause death or markedly unpleasant symptoms when taken in a moderate overdosage. Actually, the amount of either of the pills she took perhaps would not have harmed her, but the two types of antidepressant pills she took sometimes have a grave reaction when taken concomitantly. By the time her husband arrived Francine was semistuporous, trembling and gasping for air. She had tried to call a doctor or an ambulance, but the receiver had slipped out of her hand, and it hung dangling at the end of its cord. She managed to tell her husband what she had done and begged him to rush her to the hospital. Before the ambulance arrived she had a convulsion. In the ambulance on the way to the hospital she had two more convulsions. After the second convulsion she vomited her breakfast and in her semistuporous condition she inspirated large clots of half-digested food into her bronchial tubes and lungs. Her lung passages became obstructed, and she became purple as she gasped for air, her eyes bulging in terror through the mist of her semistupor. By the time she reached the hospital she was dead. The stratagem of Torture Rack was over. Francine had taken a badly Miscalculated Risk.

10

————— ··❖·· —————

Psychiatric Treatment
Maneuvers and Stratagems

Maneuvers and stratagems are so pervasive in life that they even occur in psychiatric treatment, the process which is designed to eliminate them. The patient may use maneuvers and stratagems or the psychiatrist may use them. However, a crucial factor in the maneuvers and stratagems which occur in psychiatric treatment is that the psychiatrist is aware of any stratagems he is using, and he attempts to help the patient understand and resolve any stratagems which the patient is employing.

Nevertheless, despite the knowledge of the psychiatrist and despite the efforts of the patient to get well, maneuvers and stratagems may flourish in psychiatric treatment. As the years go by, psychiatric treatment is being more widely accepted, and the stratagems which occur in it are on the increase. We shall devote this chapter to considering a few of the more common maneuvers and stratagems which occur in psychiatric treatment or as the result of it.

Most of those we shall discuss in this chapter are put-off maneuvers and stratagems, since in one way or another they defeat the purpose of psychiatric treatment. They thus prevent the patient from resolving put-off forces within himself which are disturbing his interpersonal relationships with important people in his life. However, in our discussion of Maneuvers and Stratagems Psychiatrists Carry Out with Patients we shall mention some maneuvers and stratagems which have come-on forces, since the psychiatrist is using tactics which help the patient in his total life adjustment, even though these tactics are not resolving the particular problems for which the patient consulted him.

I'm in Analysis, You Know

Psychiatric treatment means different things to different patients. To some it is a way to find relief from painful distress, to others an adventure in self-understanding and to others an escape from crippling personality limitations. But for some, it is a stratagem that carries prestige, and they vaunt their psychotherapy as a status symbol to friends and strangers alike. One of the characteristics of this group is the frequent comment "I'm in analysis, you know," or some variation of it. This is code language for saying, "I can afford it, and I have just enough problems to be fascinating but not enough to be miserable. I also have lots of superior insights into myself and other people which ordinary [unanalyzed] people do not have. In short, I am an interesting person with a superior status. I'm in analysis, you know."

One of the characteristics of these strategists is the way they throw the word "analysis" around. Analysis properly means an intense, prolonged type of interview treatment which explores the early life experiences of the patient as well as his current problems. However, the accomplished strategist of I'm in Analysis, You Know is not held down by such a rigorous definition. Any kind of contact with a psychiatrist will do. I recall a lady who saw me for two diagnostic sessions, canceled her next appointment and never saw me again. About six months later, and occasionally for several years thereafter, I ran into people who mentioned seeing my patient Mrs. Jones. From them I learned that she regularly referred to me as "my analyst" and spoke of her contacts with me as "my analysis with Dr. Chapman." Although she never went into detail about this analysis, she left the impression that most of her life decisions and behavior patterns were the product of her analysis. She justified all her acts, especially the erratic ones, as being "the sort of thing my analyst said was healthy." This lady was an unpleasant advertisement for me, since she obviously was immature, impulsive, and insensitive to the needs of others. She barged ahead to satisfy her own desires and justified her acts as the result of her analysis. One of the difficulties in being a psychiatrist is that patients can quote us but professional ethics gag us into silence.

I recall another man whom I never saw professionally but whom I knew as an acquaintance; after a few drinks at a party he cornered me and unburdened himself of some of his feelings. For years afterward he referred to me as his analyst. This was embarrassing since he was an alcoholic, and his flagrant alcoholism was obvious to most of the people who knew him. People occasionally would say to me, "You know, Doctor, your patient Don Brown is drinking again," as if they were giving me a helpful piece of advice to aid me in my analysis of Mr. Brown. On such occasions, professional ethics allowed me to say, "Mr. Brown is not and never has been a patient of mine, though I am aware that he sometimes gives a different impression." Professional ethics do not allow us to say anything about patients we have seen, but they allow us to say whom we have *not* seen.

Another characteristic of the players of this stratagem is the casual way they continually mention their analysis. "I can't meet you Wednesday at three. That's one of the days I go to see my analyst." Of course, the patient may be seeing a psychiatrist only in supportive contacts once a month, but she makes the most of every appointment in letting people know when The Day occurs. She leaves the impression that a fair part of her daylight life is spent rushing to and from the analyst's office. If some puzzled or annoyed soul asks just how often she sees this analyst, the patient replies,

"It varies depending on my needs and the work we're doing." Other comments which are dropped at parties are: "I ran into Jane when I was on my way back from [or going to] a session with my analyst." "I'm taking my vacation in July, because that's when my analyst goes out of town." "I'll have lots of time between the tenth of December and the first of the year, because we're taking a brief break in my analysis." All these comments arouse the curiosity of friends who think, "I wonder why Margaret goes to a psychiatrist; she looks all right to me." In time the strategist's friends conclude (as she wants them to conclude), "Well, I guess she can afford that sort of thing, and, with a full-time maid she probably has nothing else to do." One of the strategist's favorite tactics is to say, "We really can't afford it, you know, but I get so much out of my analysis." This remark really means, "It's dreadfully expensive and of course we *can* afford it since I *do* go to it." Such remarks are doubly impressive when the patient is driving a new sports car or is wearing expensive clothing.

The cocktail party is an ideal environment for analysis-dropping. The conversation flows high as the alcohol runs freely. Everyone is well dressed and out to impress the others, and a person often has enough anonymity in the cocktail crowd to give him ample opportunity for I'm in Analysis, You Know. For example, this maneuver can be used to open a flirtation with comments such as "You remind me so much of my analyst," or "I get more out of a talk with you than a session with my analyst," or "I think you're just what my analyst is recommending for me." The coy look, the Mona Lisa smile and the analysis maneuver start off a cocktail party flirtation that can lead to the bedroom, the altar, or both. Moreover, a large section of the public think that psychiatry preaches sexual uninhibitedness, so that the appropriate flaunting of I'm in Analysis, You Know comes across as "I've solved all those old-fashioned problems which lead to sexual inhibitions, so I'm available and quite delicious in bed." Oh, Sigmund, Sigmund, the things that are done in thy name!

In other instances, the stratagem of I'm in Analysis, You Know gives the strategist a license to begin to "analyze" friends, relatives, national political figures and anyone else. The strategist proceeds authoritatively in these analyses since he presumably has the superior insights which analysis has given him for viewing all aspects of human behavior. Moreover, since only a relatively small percentage of the population is in analysis, a skillful strategist has a conversational advantage over other people. Some strategists execute this maneuver so well that in time their friends come to them for advice on personal problems. In this way the strategist may develop a small clinical practice in her social circle. These people do less harm than would be expected, for their listeners accept the advice that sounds reasonable (or which agrees with what they already think) and ignore the rest. However, some of these veterans of analysis cause a certain amount of confusion, especially when they preach sexual release or when they advise their friends on how to rear their children.

The stratagem of I'm in Analysis, You Know is especially popular among young social workers, young psychologists, and young psychiatrists. It also is fashionable in artistic groups, amateur-theater groups and scattered nuclei of the suburban intelligentsia. In these groups the strategists sometimes collide with each other and have a battle of "My analyst is better than your analyst" or "My analyst can outanalyze your analyst any old day of the week." Favorite maneuvers in this battle are: "That's an interesting point which my analyst makes in one of his books." "Yes, I know. My analyst stressed that point in a paper he presented at the orthopsychiatry meeting in Boston three years ago." "I'd like you to read Dr. Shafer's new book. I can see so many things from my own analysis in it that I almost feel he's talking about me"; (this is the I'm Advancing Science ploy of the I'm in Analysis, You Know stratagem).

Another frequent technique is for the strategist to boast about how long his analyst's waiting list is and how many scores of suffering people are waiting to see him and simply won't see anyone else. The implication is, of course, that "my analyst" is the best since he has the longest waiting list. Some strategists carry this ploy to such an extreme that one gets the impression that an analyst's reputation is dependent not on the number of patients he treats but on the number of patients he doesn't treat. In former decades, a good strategist of I'm in Analysis, You Know frequently commented on the "charming Viennese accent of my analyst" even though the analyst was from Berlin, Budapest or Hamburg. Now that the older generation of foreign-born analysts are retiring or dying, one hears this ploy less commonly.

In former years another good tactic in this stratagem was to drop the bombshell that "my analyst was analyzed by Freud," but time has just about terminated that precious weapon. Minor variations are trotted out, however, such as "My analyst met Anna Freud and she's the most charming woman." If the strategist has by any chance met a distinguished psychiatrist, even for a one-minute introduction, the killing blow is: "You'd really enjoy knowing Franz [most distinguished psychiatrists are called Franz, Fritz, Hans or Max by people who drop their names casually in conversations] So-and-So. He's just the kind of person you'd like." A good thrust in fighting My Analyst Is Better Than Your Analyst is: "Oh, yes, I know Mr. Brown [the prominent banker, writer, industrialist or playboy]; I often run into him in my analyst's reception room. His hour is just before mine." A few well-chosen blows like this leave the impression that "my analyst" spends all his time treating the financial, social and intellectual elite of the community, including, of course, the speaker himself.

When skillful strategists of I'm in Analysis, You Know collide with each other at parties they often skirmish in a duel of I Can Outanalyze You. Each one tries to top the other's last remark as they show how profound their understanding of anyone and everyone is. Typical jabs and stabs are: "Well, of course, but behind all this is his unresolved Oedipal turmoil." "Yes, I know, but that is overshadowed by his basic anal fixation." "However, the fundamental problem is the oral deprivation which lies beneath all this other material." Each strategist maneuvers to show that his opponent is dealing only with superficial things while he has the true insight into more basic problems. They go on and on until they end up in the uterine cavity, from which point they can go no further, unless they plummet into Jung's collective racial unconscious, which, however, is sadly out of fashion.

Once they have plunged as far as the uterine cavity, they obviously must seek new areas of competitive exploration. They usually begin to quote the psychiatric literature to each other. "Have you read Freud's Schreber case? Well, you really ought to read it." This gives the strategist a wonderful opportunity to annihilate his opponent. He goes into the Schreber case in detail, and since the opponent hasn't read it he can play high and wide with any details he can't quite remember. He can douse his opponent with the Schreber case, wring him out with the Schreber case, and then hose him down again with it. An even cleverer way to open this ploy is to ask, "Have you read the Schreber case *lately?*" Then, even if his opponent has read the Schreber case, he is still one up on him since he read it only last week. A good strategist always has one old book and one new one at his fingertips. He brandishes an old book that no one reads or a new book that no one has had a chance to read yet. Thus armed, he first bludgeons his opponent with "Are you familiar with Pierre Janet's *The Major Symptoms of Hysteria* [old book which nobody reads and therefore cannot combat] or Morton Prince's study on multiple personalities [unavailable except in the basement stacks of medical school libraries]?" This maneuver dashes the opponent's weapon out of his hand, and the victorious strategist can slice him to shreds at leisure. When using a new book as a weapon, the strategist inquires, "Have you read Montgomery and Shapiro's new book?" As the opponent fumbles, obviously not even having heard of this latest piece of "publish or perish" balderdash from a couple of assistant professors who want to be chairmen of departments someday, the strategist gives him the "Oh, you poor benighted, unwashed heathen" look and beats him with a rubber hose while he quivers, paralyzed.

However, a really good strategist knows how to handle these attacks. If his opponent asks if he has read an old book, the strategist replies, "No, because that material has been outdated by later work. If you've read Black's book on that subject you're familiar with current concepts in the field." On the other hand, if his opponent asks about a new book, the skillful strategist parries by saying, "No, no. I find it's better to have a grasp of the established, proved material rather than to keep up with each new wave of froth that comes along." When two good strategists of I Can Outanalyze You get together for a battle, the spectacle can be exhilarating.

Of course, the I'm in Analysis, You Know operator also can use this stratagem as the initial move in other stratagems which we have discussed in previous chapters. He seizes an initial advantage by claiming, as the result of his analysis, "I have insights and wisdom you don't have, so my point of view must prevail." With the increase of psychotherapy in recent times, I'm in Analysis, You Know, whether used as a stratagem in itself or as the opening move in other stratagems, is becoming more prevalent. More techniques undoubtedly will be developed to enhance the armamentarium of this increasingly popular stratagem.

The irony of I'm in Analysis, You Know is that the person who is using his psychotherapy as a social stratagem actually may get a lot out of his treatment. In fact, many persons go through a phase of I'm in Analysis, You Know during the early stages of psychotherapy and then drop it as they really begin to benefit from the therapeutic experience. These benign, transitory stratagems of I'm in Analysis, You Know often may be considered par for the course. Other patients become so enraptured with the stratagem of I'm in Analysis, You Know that it becomes a major obstacle to successful treatment; they may even drop the treatment and go on with the stratagem as an end in itself. It gradually shades off into I've Been Analyzed, You Know and becomes a lifelong stratagem.

The Eternal Patient: Stratagems That Patients Execute with Psychiatrists

In occasional instances psychotherapy becomes a duel in which the patient carries out maneuvers and stratagems to obstruct treatment and to cling to the gratifications he receives from being "sick, sick, sick." Resistances to self-knowledge and exploration of painful emotional experiences occur to some extent in all treatment. But in the Eternal Patient, stratagems dominate treatment from the beginning. In the end, the patient prevails, departs in triumph, and may seek another psychiatrist. Over a period of years such patients may go through a gamut of psychiatrists whom they meet, battle and overcome. This phenomenon may be labeled Tandem Psychiatrist. Of course, the patient's stratagem is self-defeating, since he does not solve whatever problems he has. However, the gratifications which these patients get out of their symptoms are more attractive to them than the premiums of getting well. Many of them do not suffer in the usual sense of the word. The stratagem's the thing, and their particular symptoms or problems are merely foils they use in it. We shall consider a few of the common maneuvers and stratagems of the Eternal Patient.

Cure Me If You Can

In this stratagem the patient gets an exhilarating sense of superiority out of obstructing the psychiatrist's efforts to help him. The patient usually is a hostile person whose hostility is hidden beneath a façade of passive sweetness. For the first few weeks or months of treatment the patient may present a model-patient appearance. He talks spontaneously about himself and his problems and seems to be making progress. Then the patient's behavior in treatment begins to change. His attitude quickly becomes: "Well, I've done my part. Now cure me if you can." He complains increasingly about his symptoms and presses the therapist to relieve him of them. He comments on how other people "get helped" and he presses the therapist to "help me too." The patient reports lack of improvement, or perhaps deterioration, in his condition at every session. If the therapist is inexperienced he makes extraordinary efforts for the patient. The patient responds to these special efforts by reporting triumphantly that he is doing even worse than before. As the therapist squirms, the patient puts more and more pressure on him to "help me because I'm suffering so much." Finally, treatment ends in a stalemate with the therapist dejected and defeated. The victorious patient leaves the field with his symptoms intact for any later encounters with other psychiatrists.

These patients have profound hostility in most of their interpersonal relationships, and they execute obstructing stratagems in their marriages, their work situations, their relationships with their children, and so forth. Cure Me If You Can is the particular stratagem they work on psychiatrists. The proper way for the psychiatrist to deal with this stratagem is to attempt to explore the hostility which the patient is expressing by clinging to his symptoms and obstructing treatment. However, the patient often evades, overleaps or smashes down such attempts. I recall a patient with whom I attempted to begin to explore the hostility that lay behind his role in treatment. He was a polite, dignified economist who behaved with meticulous self-control most of the time. When I made a general comment about the possible hostility that lay behind his behavior in treatment, he flushed red in the face, shook his finger at me and shouted, "I never get angry at anybody. Don't you dare ever say such a thing to me again."

Some patients devise ingenious ways to taunt and defeat the psychiatrist. I remember an alcoholic suburban lady who brought a can of beer to each session and sipped it during the hour. "You know I need this stuff and can't do without it, Doctor," she explained as she stretched out in her chair and put the can down. She periodically wiped up the rings which the can made on the table and smiled sweetly as she said, "I hope it doesn't mark up the table top." When I finally tried to approach the taunting hostility in this act, she smiled with obvious satisfaction and replied, "Why, Doctor, that's what you're supposed to be curing me of," and she thereupon took a large swig out of the can.

Another young lady came dutifully to the sessions and inquired what I wanted her to do to get well. I indicated that she should talk about her feelings and her life. She inquired if she might talk about anything that came to mind. I replied that she might begin that way. She then pulled out the morning newspaper and spent forty-five minutes reading an article on political and economic conditions in central Europe. She then used the last five minutes to press me to help her "now that I've done my part" and complained that she was not making progress in treatment. She was twenty-six years old and I was the fifth psychiatrist she had seen. I am sure there were others after me.

Poor Little Me

In this stratagem the patient's theme is: "I could get well if only it weren't for . . ." The patient, in veiled or direct ways, says, "I could get well, Doctor, if only you could do something about my husband," or "if we had more money," or "if you could do something about my mother," and so forth. During the housing shortage after the Second World War a common theme was: "if only we had a place of our own, away from my folks," or "if we only had a decent apartment." In most of these situations the psychiatrist can do nothing about the patient's husband (who may or may not need something done to him), her mother (who lives in another city), her economic situation (which may be satisfactory), or her housing situation (which she may evade resolving by finding endless objections to every new apartment that is available). If the therapist attempts to intervene directly in any of these problems, instead of dealing with the patient's gratifications in hanging onto her problems and using the stratagem of Poor Little Me, she traps him into an awkward effort that is doomed to failure. She then sinks into an even more entrenched role of Poor Little Me. "Even a psychiatrist couldn't solve my problems. How can you expect me to?"

Let You and Them Fight

In this stratagem the Eternal Patient tries to manipulate the psychiatrist into championing him in his struggles with members of his family. He pitches the psychiatrist into battle with his relatives, and then he settles back to watch the fray. The picture the patient presents of his relatives may be valid, partially valid or completely false; usually it is one of the last two. In these cases, no real treatment goes on at all. The patient retires from treatment and watches the debacle of the therapist's misadventure with the relatives. An experienced therapist does not fall into this trap. He emphasizes to the patient that he must solve his personality problems first and then he will be able to make the best possible arrangements with his family. The psychiatrist is the patient's therapist, not his knight on a white charger to do battle for him.

If I Only Had a Better Therapist

In this stratagem the Eternal Patient's theme is: "If I only had a better therapist I could get well." This stratagem may be executed in any kind of clinical setting. In a medical-school clinic or any other situation where patients are seen at reduced fees to meet the patient's economic circumstances, the patient may inquire, "If I could afford to go to a regular, experienced private doctor, do you think it would help?" The implication is: "If I had a real doctor instead of an amateur, do you think my suffering might end?" Some patients become very skillful at crushing therapists with this maneuver and derive much satisfaction in it.

Another delicious stab is: "It's nothing against you personally, Doctor, that you aren't experienced enough to help me, but . . ." and then the patient goes on to tell the doctor how much he's suffering as the result of the doctor's inadequacies. "Doctor, have you ever treated a case like mine before? Have you been in this kind of work very long? Well, I guess they always say a new broom sweeps clean. . . ." "Doctor, I'm sure both of us would like to see at least a little progress in my case. It must be discouraging to a young man like you to see me no better week after week." Some of these strategists take a head-patting, patronizing attitude: "I know your mother must be proud of you that you became a doctor," or "You young doctors work so hard to get your training. Are you still in your training, or are you fully qualified?"

In private-practice situations, these able strategists cut their doctors down to size in other ways. "Dr. Jones charges his patients five dollars an hour more than you do, but I can't afford that, so I'll have to stick with you." "Do you think I should go to a university medical center where they will have the facilities to understand my case, or do you think we should plod along as we're going?"

"I hear that Dr. Blue is a fully trained psychiatrist who studied eight years in Boston. Do you think that such a better-trained man would be better for me?" I had one lady who assaulted me directly with the inquiry "Doctor, why isn't your office out farther in the suburbs where all the good psychiatrists are?" Another patient sympathetically consoled me, "I guess the overhead is less down here, but when you're better established you can move out farther." Cutting the psychiatrist down is such an exhilarating sport that the Eternal Patient sometimes abandons the central work of treatment to engage in psychiatrist-baiting much of the time.

Maneuvers and Stratagems Psychiatrists Carry Out with Patients

In the preceding parts of this chapter we have considered stratagems that patients execute with psychiatrists. In these situations the psychiatrist tries to help the patient develop insight into how he uses these stratagems both in treatment and in relationships with other people outside treatment. The patient has carried into stratagems with the psychiatrist the unresolved emotional problems which arose originally in previous relationships in his life.

We now come to the maneuvers and stratagems that psychiatrists carry out with the patients. A crucial factor in these stratagems is that the psychiatrist knows that he is executing a stratagem. The patient may or may not understand the psychiatrist's stratagem. Many times he dimly perceives it but does not want to understand it better, and the psychiatrist may not press the point. Usually, the psychiatrist is forced to use these stratagems with patients who must be treated but who technically are untreatable; they must have psychiatric treatment but are unlikely to make progress in it. Some of these patients are more or less normal, but they have urgent reasons why they must have psychiatric treatment. In short, they cannot benefit from treatment as such, but other aspects of treatment are necessary for them. For humane reasons, but not for valid scientific ones, the psychiatrist must sigh and resign himself to treating them. These patients, of course, constitute only a tiny fraction of patients seen in psychiatric practice. We shall discuss a few of them.

I recall a thirty-two-year-old attractive mother of two children whose anguished husband brought her for psychiatric treatment after he discovered that she had had a brief extramarital affair with a business colleague of his. The husband was in love with his wife and had considered his home happy until this occurred. He said with much agitation, "She must be sick, Doctor, very sick, or she wouldn't have done a thing like this. She needs treatment, not a divorce." I spent four sessions examining her carefully. She was not really sick. She was the somewhat indulged, only daughter of doting parents who had allowed her to do whatever she wanted and to have her own way on everything. She had developed into a charming, vivacious girl who had had many boyfriends and several affairs before she married. She had a thread of self-centered willfulness in her personality which, however, was not marked enough to cast her outside the boundaries of normality. She got along well with her husband and was a good mother and wife. However, while her husband was out of town on business she had a brief affair with a business colleague of his; the man had taken the initiative, but the excitement of the idea swept her along on this extramarital adventure. After three rendezvous with the man she cut the affair off and had no emotional investment in it. However, her husband a short time later discovered what had happened when a friend of his told him he had seen his wife and the other man checking out of a motel.

The husband was faced with an agonizing dilemma. His self-respect and pride made it difficult for him to continue the marriage after what had happened. However, he would be miserable to lose the wife he loved and the home and children he adored. His wife was equally anxious to preserve the marriage and quietly admitted to me that she had been "a little fool," since her husband was "twice the man" the other man was and a very good provider. The anguished husband consulted a friend who, in despair, suggested that maybe she was "sick." The husband grasped this straw and his wife readily went along with the idea. So they consulted me.

She was not really "sick"; I knew it and she knew I knew it. Moreover, she did not feel she was sick. Neither of us pressed the point, however. We both knew that she must be "treated" to save her marriage and to preserve the happiness of her husband and her children. I had a choice; I could be a scientist and damage them all by saying she did not need psychotherapy, or I could be humane and say that "this situation merits treatment, and beneficial results will come of it." To preserve the shreds of my professional honesty, my phraseology was somewhat tortuous. "The situation [not the patient] merits treatment" and "beneficial results will come of it [not by any change in the patient's personality structure, but by saving the marriage and the happiness of four people]."

So the patient and I settled down to a treatment stratagem. Both of us knew that no treatment was going on, although neither one of us ever said so. She played the role of a patient very obligingly. She made little notes before each session and once a week talked for fifty minutes about her childhood, her adolescence, her courtship and her marriage. She dutifully reported her dreams and I made some bland interpretations about them which she said were "very interesting and original." I made "interpretations" from time to time.

After six months of this stratagem, she told me she thought she was doing well and wondered when we could stop. I indicated I felt that "things were much better" and that we might talk about stopping. I asked if she had talked with her husband about terminating treatment. She replied that she had done so and that he told her, "The doctor has done wonders for you. You are a different person." I saw the husband briefly and he expressed much gratitude for all I had done for his wife. In my final session with the wife soon afterward, I indicated that I felt "treatment had served a very useful purpose," but I emphasized that any repetition of the "precipitating stress" might not be so easily resolved a second time. Her discreet smile and assurances that she "had learned a lot in treatment" indicated that she understood quite well what I meant. Eight years have passed since I last saw this lady, and the fact that I have had no further word from this couple probably means that "treatment was successful." Fortunately, my monthly statements read only "For professional services" and state the amount due. An itemized statement in this case would have to read "For saving your marriage by executing a good stratagem," and doctors just can't send out statements like that.

A treatment stratagem sometimes is executed with a young homosexual who gets caught in a homosexual act by school authorities or by the indignant relatives of another man with whom the homosexual is involved. For example, I recall a twenty-five-year-old graduate student who had only eight months more work before receiving his Ph.D. when he was caught by university officials in a homosexual relationship with a twenty-four-year-old friend of his. He was brought before the dean of the graduate school, who expelled him. Faced with the loss of all credits for his graduate education and with poor possibilities of ever being admitted to another graduate school, he desperately begged the dean to allow him to see if he could solve his problem by treatment. This gave the dean, who was glad to find some way to be more lenient, a way out, and the dean agreed to suspend him, subject to readmission if he were in psychiatric treatment.

Homosexuals who are pushed into psychiatric treatment by situational pressures rarely change their sexual orientation. I knew this, and the graduate student knew it. However, both he and I knew that three percent of the adult population is homosexual, but that few of them are so cruelly punished for their problems as he was in danger of being punished. For humane reasons, but not for valid scientific ones, I "treated" him. He was a dutiful patient; he attended his sessions and talked spontaneously. In time he was readmitted to graduate school with a letter from me stating that he was "attending treatment sessions regularly once a week," and eventually he received his degree. After that, "treatment" withered and died. Early in my career I "treated" several other homosexuals in similar predicaments, but I grew tired of the stratagem, and I was not entirely comfortable with my conscience about it. In recent years I have sent them all to younger colleagues for "treatment." Some of my younger colleagues go at these patients with considerable vigor and self-assurance that they are going to change them. The patients and I know better; we've heard about maneuvers and stratagems.

A variety of other types of patients occasionally appear in psychiatrists' offices needing treatment despite the fact that they are either untreatable or normal. For example, a psychiatrist occasionally sees an erring husband whose wife has discovered him in an extramarital affair and she tearfully brings him in for treatment "to save our home"; we usually save the home. Fifty years ago these men were carted to clergymen who "redeemed them," "cleansed them," or "saved them." Today the average suburban American turns to science rather than to religion for this service, but the end result, at least as far as "saving the home" is concerned, is the same. Science costs more than religion, but we are said to be living in the affluent society.

An adolescent girl whose parents discover her in a sexual affair sometimes is brought for psychiatric treatment. She must be cleansed somehow or other, or her parents cannot look at her comfortably across the breakfast table. Some of these girls need treatment and benefit from it. Some of them need treatment but will not really engage in it. They only execute a treatment stratagem for a while to make living together emotionally possible for them and their parents. In our culture sexual intercourse is a treatable condition in adolescent girls, but not in adolescent boys.

Of course, we psychiatrists sometimes are wrong. In a number of cases in which I thought I was engaged in a treatment stratagem I discovered that the patient was having a valid treatment experience. Halfway through the treatment the patient more or less said, "I'm through with this stratagem; let's settle down and get to work." This is the most valid justification for the stratagems that psychiatrists carry out with patients; they sometimes lead to something more useful than mere stratagems.

Pill Maneuvers and Stratagems

Most psychiatrists feel that with the majority of patients the role of medications in psychiatric treatment should be carefully defined as helping to make the patient more comfortable while he is working in interviews to resolve his emotional problems. A few medications, such as the phenothiazines in schizophrenia and some of the antidepressants in depressions, may play more decisive roles, but for the vast majority of patients treated in office practice, medications can at best be only secondary aids.

A few patients find stratagems to carry out with any factor which is used in psychiatric practice. Hence, we have pill maneuvers and stratagems. In a pill stratagem a patient may manipulate the pill in his relationship with the psychiatrist, or he may take the pill off to operate a stratagem alone by himself. For example, a patient who becomes addicted to sedatives excludes the psychiatrist and executes a solitary stratagem in which his relationship with the pill becomes more important to him than any of his interpersonal relationships. In a pill stratagem the patient corrupts the use of the medication in some way, so that it becomes a weapon against the psychiatrist or a substitute for him.

Magic Pill

Some patients invest a medication with such impressive powers that they soon can dispense with the psychiatrist altogether. This phenomenon is illustrated by a forty-five-year-old accountant who consulted me for severe insomnia of one year's duration. I explained that while we were working on his emotional problems I would give him a prescription for some sleeping pills to give him temporary relief. He kept one more appointment, canceled the following one, and never came again. Two years later, at ten o'clock one night, I received a call from him. "Doctor," he cried, "I've just discovered that I left my sleeping pills in a hotel room in Cincinnati; I was there on business and flew back into town this afternoon. I won't be able to sleep without them." After making sure who he was, I asked in amazement if he was still taking the pills. "No, no," he replied, "I never took them. I got the prescription filled and then put the bottle on the dresser, knowing that if I didn't sleep I could take one. Then I went to sleep. I've kept them with me ever since, and I never had to take one. But now, I left them in Cincinnati and I know I won't be able to sleep tonight." I telephoned a prescription to a drugstore which supplied him with five of the pills, and I suggested that he see me further in the office. He never came and he still may be toting his five Magic Pills around. In this case the patient substituted the Magic Pill for the doctor. One of the troubles with the Magic Pill is that its effect usually wears off in time. However, for some patients the magical influence works for years or decades. I have seen patients who functioned fairly well on medications prescribed by doctors who had been dead for years. The idea of being without the Magic Pill (usually something that could be got without a prescription) terrified them.

226

Talisman

A talisman is an object of some sort that a person carries with him at all times to protect him from evil. The proverbial rabbit's foot carried in the hip pocket to ward off bad luck was a typical talisman in former times; some people wouldn't go out of the house without it. Pills may act the same way. The pill becomes the patient's protector against symptoms, terror and misfortunes. So long as he carries the medication with him he feels safe. Without it he feels defenseless and in danger; a wave of anxiety comes over him. The patient may or may not take the Talisman pill. He may take one or two of them at regular times during the day or he may merely carry them with him at all times. Many pills used in this way are of such small dosage that they have negligible pharmacologic effect.

Talisman pills are employed in a light stratagem with the doctor. They almost become a substitute for him, but not quite. To maintain the effect of the pills, the patient must have occasional contacts with the doctor from once every few weeks to once every six months. Hence, Talisman stratagems usually are executed with family doctors or internists, but patients sometimes inveigle this stratagem out of a psychiatrist. The pill becomes a symbol of the doctor's protecting power, and the patient can, in a sense, carry a tangible piece of the doctor with him.

Talisman stratagems are common in patients with phobias, such as fears of going into crowds or into small rooms. I recall a patient whom I thought I cured of a phobia by psychotherapy, and I feel it did help her. However, years later I met this patient socially and was chagrined when she said, "You know, Doctor, wherever I go I still carry with me those pills you gave me. I never take them, but I feel better if I have them with me, just in case."

The Talisman stratagem has a consoling feature for the psychiatrist. After I am dead, a certain number of people for years afterward will still carry talismans of me, in the form of pills. In symbolic form, I shall be "treating" them even though I have departed from this world. All of us long for a little physical immortality. We all like to leave something behind, even if it's only a Talisman stratagem.

Side Reaction

Some hostile, deprecating patients like to box their doctors into corners and then cut them down to size with Side Reaction. The stratagem proceeds as follows: Mrs. Mad complains pressingly to her doctor, who may be her family doctor or her psychiatrist, about certain symptoms, such as anxiety, headaches or fatigue. She inquires, "Certainly you can prescribe something to give me a little relief?" He does. She now has him just where she wants him, and she can cut him down to size and show him how inadequate a doctor he is, damaging people when he should be helping them. The next day, or late the same night, Dr. Gullible gets a telephone call from Mrs. Mad or her husband. "Doctor, you remember the pills you gave me. Well, I'm having a terrible side reaction to them. I feel terrible . . ." and a long list of symptoms follows. The doctor usually tells her to stop taking them. However, the symptoms go on the next day and the doctor receives two or three more telephone calls. In desperation he prescribes something else, and even worse side reactions follow. The patient now has the doctor in a trap. If he doesn't give her medication she suffers agony with her symptoms, and if he does give her medication she suffers agony with side reactions. The wary doctor quickly sees the stratagem she is setting up with him, and he frankly tells the patient and her family that in his opinion both the patient's original symptoms and her side reactions are caused mainly by emotional factors; he indicates that more pills will not help the situation. This ends the stratagem. The patient may settle down to psychotherapy with a psychiatrist at this point, but more often she goes shopping for another physician with whom she can execute this stratagem for weeks, months or years.

The physician who gets firmly caught in a stratagem of Side Reaction has a bad time of it. Finally, he and the patient decide that the patient must go to the hospital to find out what's going on. Then the patient tells everyone that the doctor's medicine made her "so sick that it put me in the hospital." Needless to say, all laboratory tests which involve swallowing anything or having anything injected into her lead to more side reactions. The patient nails the squirming doctor to the wall and shows everyone how inadequate and blundering he is. Some hostile women get so much gratification from this stratagem that they execute it for years, usually with a chain of doctors. These patients usually become famous in the local medical community.

Compensation Stratagems

Our troubled era has been called a lot of things. It has been called the Age of Anxiety, the Nuclear Age, the Century of the Common Man, and many other things. It might also be called the Age of Compensation.

An endless stream of people want compensation for things that have happened to them or which they allege have happened. Each year hundreds of thousands of people sue and countersue each other for damages. People who trip over rugs and people who think they tripped over rugs, people with grievances against neighbors and people who imagine they have grievances against neighbors, people with smashed fenders and people with smashed bones, people who jam their fingers in car doors and people who jam their toes in elevators, children who get bitten by dogs and dogs that get hit by cars, people unborn and people already dead—all are suing their fellow citizens, who in turn countersue them. The object of all this commotion is money. However, money is an unfashionable word and it jars the ears of jurymen. Hence, the word "money" is never used in all this scrambling. Instead, the word "compensation" is used.

The medical profession is dragged in by its ears and hauled onto the witness stand to try to describe the patient's suffering, or the absence of it, to twelve of the patient's peers. These peers, who yesterday were on a production line making washing machines or trying to keep house in the suburbs, are now called upon to decide whether or not a man sitting in the front row of a courtroom has a ruptured intervertebral disc and whether or not a collision of his automobile with another car sixteen months before then caused it. Obviously, the opportunities for stratagems, maneuvers, confusion and chaos are excellent, and Justice staggers onward while lawyers, witnesses, juries, plaintiffs, defendants and judges bludgeon her to death.

As the Age of Compensation has developed among us, psychiatry has assumed a crucial role, for many of these people have "mental suffering." Of course, the human race has had mental suffering since Eve made her gastronomic error in the Garden of Eden and Adam shared the same apple dumpling with her. However, only in our time have people been paid money for their mental suffering.

Of course, mental suffering is rather difficult to define and somewhat elusive to measure. This does not deter the able strategists who professionally calculate it in precise dollar figures. *They* know just how much mental suffering is worth $15,000 and how much is worth $50,000. They know the value of a tear, the cost of a wince, and the money equivalent of a twinge. Not only do *they* know, but washing-machine mechanics and housewives on juries also know these things. The Age of Compensation has wrought these wonders.

Money has a curious effect on the human body and the human psyche. A bruise suffered from falling off a ladder in your own home heals without much trouble in a week or so. A bruise suffered by tripping over a rug in a downtown office building often takes many weeks or months to heal because it has a devastating complication; it is compensable. A citizen rubs liniment on a homegrown bruise and lies on a heating pad. However, he goes to orthopedists for psychotherapy and X-rays for a factory-spawned bruise. People who stumble while getting out of their own cars limp for two days, but people who stumble getting out of other people's cars limp for two years. However, all this is elementary compared to compensable psychiatric problems such as "anxiety," "depressiveness" and "mental suffering" which are triggered by injuries on premises covered by liability insurance. Mental anguish is like outer space; its limits are endless.

True malingering of psychiatric symptoms is rare. The afflicted person actually feels the emotional pain, the anxiety and the other emotional symptoms he describes. However, money has a major role in turning symptoms that otherwise would be minor and transitory into severe, prolonged disabilities. Moreover, the suits drag on for years as lawyers bicker and try to outstare each other, and the symptoms have become irreversible by the time the money is paid. The patient continues to have his suffering for years or decades afterward. I have seen patients who were still having their symptoms ten to twenty years after their compensation was finally settled.

On a number of occasions a lawyer has told me, "Doctor, we just want an evaluation of the patient. That's all." When I suggested that it also would be a good idea to treat the patient, he replied, "Well, we can wait for that until after the case is settled." One of them frankly told me that if the patient got well it would hurt the suit or perhaps annihilate it altogether. "Then," he continued, "none of us would get paid for all our services to the patient, would we, Doctor?"

231

A compensation stratagem is a conspiracy on a wide scale. The plaintiff's lawyer gets paid out of the plaintiff's compensation for representing him. The attorneys for the defendant (usually an insurance company) get paid for battling for the defendant. Technical experts, various physicians and psychiatrists are paid for their examinations and their testimony time on the witness stand. Secretaries, typists, court clerks, court reporters, jurymen and the people who polish the courtroom floors at night also receive money. The patient usually gets something at the end, although as a rule not as much as he hoped. On the surface, the compensation stratagem supports more people in a more affluent way than any other stratagem we have considered. Indeed, one wonders why this marvelous economic invention was not discovered centuries ago; it helps so many people.

However, the laws of thermodynamics state that energy is neither created nor destroyed, and the same principle applies to stratagems. Somebody pays for all this. The payment usually is delayed. It comes at two o'clock in the morning in darkened bedrooms for years and perhaps decades afterward, as a voice says, "Mary, will you get me the heating pad and two more of those pills? I haven't been able to sleep yet, with all this pain in my legs and back."

Shakespeare said of money, "This yellow slave will knit and break religions." He hadn't heard about compensation stratagems.

11

Maneuvers and Stratagems
of Social Groups

In the preceding chapters of this book we have dealt with the maneuvers and stratagems which occur between individuals. In the present chapter we shall consider how a few of these same maneuvers and stratagems may occur between different groups in society.

For example, Social Group A may carry out a stratagem to force Social Group B into some sort of action or to accomplish some specific goal. The stratagem may or may not work, and it may or may not be in the long-range best interests of either or both groups. Group A also may not have clear awareness of just why it is doing what it is doing, and often its true motivations are hidden by a camouflage of rationalizations. The stratagem usually proceeds out of an unhealthy social situation and its results often are unhealthy for both groups and for society as a whole. If the group's activity is brief and limited, it may be termed a maneuver; if it is prolonged and massive, it is a stratagem. Usually the majority of the social body is not directly involved as Groups A and B become locked in their stratagem, but the interests of the uninvolved segments of society usually are hurt by the struggle. However, some stratagems are so large that most of the social structure is involved in them at least part of the time. We shall examine a few of the stratagems between social groups which may lead to civil unrest or a disruption of healthy social and economic patterns. All the stratagems we shall examine are put-off stratagems; they are motivated by hostile, competitive forces between social groups, and they shove social groups apart from one another.

Temper Tantrum

Temper Tantrum, described as a child-parent stratagem in Chapter 4, occurs in a situation in which one group, Group A, feels itself deprived of things possessed by the larger, more powerful group, Group B. Group A wants some of these things and feels frustrated that Group B has not arranged for them to have them. Group A feels deprived and angry; it has protested and howled to a certain extent, but Group B has ignored the howling and protesting. Group A simmers, and then one night it executes Temper Tantrum. Just as a child in Temper Tantrum throws himself down, thrashes, kicks, bites and may destroy some furniture or bric-a-brac in his Temper Tantrum, Group A shouts, howls, thrashes, runs wild and destroys things. Just as the child accomplishes nothing immediately in his Temper Tantrum, Group A accomplishes nothing immediately but expects that the commotion of Temper Tantrum will mobilize Group B into supplying its wants. Just as the child may hurt itself in Temper Tantrum, Group A may hurt itself. Group A often damages some of Group B's property and also some of its own, just as a child may kick over an end table and also smash his own toys in Temper Tantrum. Just as family Temper Tantrums are unhealthy ways to try to solve family problems, social Temper Tantrums are unhealthy ways to try to solve social problems.

A social Temper Tantrum usually begins when Group A is feeling irritable and restless. A number of recent minor frustrations have been added to its long-standing complaints. Then one hot, humid night a small frustration causes Group A to explode into Temper Tantrum. A member of Group A misbehaves. He violates a traffic regulation, or causes a disturbance while drunk, or starts a taunting brawl with other members of his own group or with members of Group B. Group B, in the person of its disciplinary force, the police, enters to stop this disturbance. The offending member of Group A fights back. He resists, curses, shouts accusations and makes much noise. A scuffle ensues between the Group A person and a few of the Group B police. Other members of Group A have heard the noise, have poked their heads out of windows and have come running. The other members of Group A are not particularly concerned with whether the unruly Group A member is right or wrong. They are swept along by their anger and frustration toward Group B and by their feeling that Group B is not coming across with what Group A wants and needs. Soon a crowd has collected and the crowd quickly becomes a mob. Then the Group A mob begins Temper Tantrum. It howls and defies Group B. It throws itself into the streets to thrash, smash and loot.

For the moment Group B is unable to control Group A's Temper Tantrum. Group A, usually led by adolescents and young adults, smashes automobiles, store windows and building fronts. It sets fires, hurls rocks, shoots guns and goes wildly rampant in the streets. It loots stores and carries off a few of the things it thinks Group B should give it. For the moment, Group A revels in the feeling that Group B cannot control Temper Tantrum, and it spreads Temper Tantrum from block to block and from one section of the city to another. In the process, as in all Temper Tantrum maneuvers, Group A hurts itself to some extent. Some of its own members are injured, and they destroy some of the shops and businesses which give them employment. The fires they set spread to their own homes and businesses, and they loot the stores of their own group.

By this time Group B realizes it has a full-fledged Temper Tantrum on its hands and must do something about it. How it handles

Temper Tantrum depends on what kind of parent Group B is. If Group B is a liberal, permissive kind of parent it procrastinates awhile, tries to reason with its rampaging child, makes threats to do something drastic if Temper Tantrum doesn't stop, and takes half-hearted punitive measures. Reassurances and discussions may work when a child is calm, but as a rule they are useless once a full-fledged Temper Tantrum has been unleashed. Finally, after hours or days of Temper Tantrum, Group B, against its liberal ideas, cracks down with force and stops Temper Tantrum. The police are reinforced, or the National Guard and other troops are called in, and Temper Tantrum stops. A few fitful, final thrashings occur, but Group B finally controls the situation. However, if Group B is an old-fashioned, "no nonsense," strict kind of parent, it is promptly indignant and horrified by Temper Tantrum, and it imposes massive force at once; after a certain amount of struggle, Temper Tantrum stops. Then everybody goes to work to clean up the debris.

There is much controversy about whether Temper Tantrum by a social group brings any benefits. Some of Group A's members feel that Temper Tantrums force Group B into doing something to redress its grievances, whereas others feel that Temper Tantrums merely make Group B mad and result in more tension. The members of Group B are equally divided. Some feel that Temper Tantrum is a sign of social unhealthiness and that something should be done to improve the general social health. Other members of Group B feel that Temper Tantrum is an immature, immoral defiance of how society should run and that prompt, massive force is the proper response to such disobedience. They feel, moreover, that making concessions to Group A after Temper Tantrum only encourages more Temper Tantrums. Many other members of both Groups A and B are puzzled and not sure. However, most people feel that Temper Tantrums are a sign of unhealthy relationships between groups in society, although there is much debate about how to correct the unhealthiness which causes them.

In some instances, Temper Tantrums are fatal to some members of both Groups A and B, and they become tragic in addition to being unhealthy and destructive.

Divide and Rule

The operation of Divide and Rule in social groups is similar to its operations in family groups, as outlined in Chapter 4. Group A wants something from Group B. Group A knows that if Group B stands united against it, it will have a much harder time getting what it wants or may not be able to get it at all. Hence, just as in a family stratagem of Divide and Rule the child divides his parents and plays them off against each other to accomplish his ends, Group A tries to divide Group B into two or more subgroups and then play them off against each other. Sometimes the stratagem works, and sometimes it does not.

Social Divide and Rule occurs classically in labor-management relations. Group A is a labor union or a group of labor unions working in the same industry. Group A wants things from Group B, which is the management and ownership of the business or businesses for whom Group A works. Group A looks at the cars Group B members drive, the houses they live in, the vacations they take, and the places they send their children to college, and decides that it is not getting its fair share of the profits of their joint enterprise. More important still, the wives of Group A think they are not getting *their* fair share, and they stimulate the male members of Group A into a state of much restlessness and agitation. Hence, when the time for contract negotiations rolls around, Group A makes a bid for more money, more fringe benefits, and more privileges. Group B agrees to a few of Group A's requests but labels the rest of them unrealistic and unjustified. A few discussions follow, a few hot words may fly, and a stalemate occurs.

Group A decides it must do something to force Group B into

coming across with what it wants. However, if it faces all the component parts of Group B at once, it may lose. Hence, it tries a Divide and Rule stratagem.

Group B is composed of three companies, the Greens, the Blues and the Yellows. Green, Blue and Yellow are archcompetitors. They fight yearly for the market and struggle to outproduce and outsell each other. They already are in a state of competitive division and Group A intends to make the most of this by a skillful stratagem of Divide and Rule. If Group A, which wants essentially the same things from all three companies, went on strike at all of them at the same time, it would lost its main advantage. Hence, if Group A can stay united and if Group B will stay disunited, a wonderful opportunity for Divide and Rule exists.

Group A has been working Divide and Rule stratagems on Group B for half a century and knows the rules. Group B ought to know the rules and defend itself better, but Companies Green, Blue and Yellow are so bitterly competitive that they can't get together to fight Group A with a solid front. From the Group A point of view, it is a good thing that they cannot.

Group A attacks Company Green first. They make their demands, which they call "humanitarian"; Green terms the demands "fantastic" and rejects them. Much talk ensues, headlines are made, and Group A goes on strike. Company Green closes down, and Group A members try to live on much less. The stockholders of Company Green are miserable as they envision reduced dividend checks with which to pay for houses already bought, college tuition for children already in college and country-club dues for country clubs already joined. Group A is restless since their wives and children have developed the inconvenient habits of liking to be well clothed, well housed, well fed, well entertained, and well up with their neighbors in all these areas. However, the strike goes on and words like "humanitarian" and "fantastic" continue to be thrown around. A government mediator suggested a compromise three weeks before the strike occurred, but the union leaders—who want to get reelected by the membership next year and must put up a good show of fighting the management—termed this compromise "disgraceful," and company officials—who want to impress the stockholders that they're fighting to keep dividends up and thus keep their jobs—called the compromise suggestions "ridiculous." So the mediator twiddles his thumbs, arranges periodic meetings between Groups A and B, and knows that when the stockholders get scared enough and the wives of the union workers get tired of the phone calls and doorbell ringings for delinquent time payments on color television sets and automobiles, both parties will accept more or less what he recommended three weeks before the strike began. The mediator has been through this stratagem many times before and knows that you cannot reason with people who use words like "humanitarian" and "fantastic." You have to wait until stark necessity forces them to do the reasonable thing.

Meanwhile, Divide and Rule is working away. While Company Green is on strike, Companies Blue and Yellow take over the market. Company Green's profits go down, and Companies Blue and Yellow gloat and hope Green's strike goes on forever. Of course, they know it won't go on forever, but that it will be settled in time and then they will get the ax. However, reason rarely prevails entirely in human affairs, and so they hope that somehow or other they will have a short strike or that some magic will happen and they will have no strike at all. Thus, Divide and Rule grinds on, and everybody is getting hurt, but everybody figures that he will be hurt less than anybody else because he is cleverer, more resourceful, and understands the situation better than the others.

Finally, after weeks of arguing, waiting and thumb-twiddling, Company Green and the unions settle for about what the mediator originally suggested. The union officials call it a "great humanitarian victory." Their members ratify the agreement because they must go home afterward and face their wives, who are tired of having them cluttering up the house all the time, and hence their marriages and their sex lives are deteriorating. So they ratify the agreement and go back to work. The company officials claim a great victory over the "unrealistic" demands of the union and somewhere in the small print mention that dividends will be smaller this year. The stockholders grind their teeth and accept it since some dividends are better than none at all.

The whole industry functions in harmony, efficiency and prosperity for ten days. Then Group A strikes at Company Blue. More talk, more use of the words "humanitarian" and "fantastic," more thumb-twiddling, more nervousness in the stockholders, more griping by workers' wives with husbands home all day or, worse still, at the neighborhood tavern, until we have another settlement with another "great humanitarian victory" and another "victory over fantastic demands." Then, after ten more days of harmony and prosperity Group A strikes Company Yellow, and the same cycle is repeated with new griping wives and new nervous stockholders.

The stratagem of Divide and Rule is now over until new contract negotiations begin again two years later. The government mediator, whose thumbs are in a raw, bleeding condition from so much thumb-twiddling, goes off to Florida for a two-week rest so that he can begin the same process over again on the fifteenth of next month. At that time he has the same situation coming up with another Group A which is all set for a good stratagem of Divide and Rule with Companies Black, White and Gray.

Peck Order

Peck Order, which is discussed in Chapter 5 as a marital stratagem, also is carried out between social groups in every nation. In social Peck Order one group works hard to demonstrate its superiority over inferior social groups, which in turn are trying to demonstrate their superiority over still lesser social groups.

No matter how egalitarian the stated aims of a nation are, it soon develops clearly defined social groups which try to show their superiority to other groups and thus establish their preeminence in the social Peck Order. For example, in Communist nations, a technological and administrative bureaucracy soon establishes itself, in addition to the governing cliques within the Communist party itself, and these social groups live more elaborately than the working classes. These groups have better apartments, color television sets and government automobiles with chauffeurs. The top Peck Order social group in a Communist nation gets its children into the universities and better government positions so it can perpetuate its superior social status from one generation to another. Below this group are the secondary social groups that assist in running the factories, collective farms and government stores. This group also has better living conditions, more luxuries and more privileges than the still lower groups. So on down the scale, the inevitable Peck Order establishes itself, while the leaders proclaim the supremacy of the proletariat and condemn all other societies for their social inequalities.

Power once grasped is clung to, and power long enjoyed leads to privileges. Within a few years a new top Peck Order group develops superior living standards and privileges. In religious history, the barefoot itinerant disciples are succeeded by prelates with splendid robes and imposing temples. In political history, each new reforming group in time establishes a new Peck Order with itself at the top, if it can. In economic and social history, each new wave of reform that sweeps away an old Peck Order slowly or rapidly builds a new one (usually while preaching that Peck-Orderism has come to an end) and jockeys itself into the top position and its dependent allies into secondary positions. Peck Order is here to stay.

However, establishing a Peck Order is not enough for the successful group. They have to show it off to other groups, even, perhaps, while proclaiming that it does not exist. In examining how they do this, we shall borrow heavily from that great student of Peck-Orderism (although he did not use the term), the astute

American economist and social observer Thorstein Veblen. Veblen himself defied the lures of Peck-Orderism very successfully; although probably the most original and distinguished economist in American history, he managed to die impoverished in a tar-paper shack in California at the age of seventy-one in 1929. Such triumphant defiance of Peck-Orderism occurs only in exceptional individuals. Society as a whole clings to its precious Peck Order, which brings it so much superficial pleasure and so much basic grief.

We shall examine in detail how the superior groups enjoy the fruits of their successful struggle in the Peck Order by making it gallingly obvious to the inferior groups.

First of all, the successful Peck Order strategists cover their bodies in stylish ways. They adorn themselves with fine fabrics of the most fashionable cuts and trim themselves with the newest kinds of ornaments. In a rational human society in which Peck Order did not exist, a few years of research and practical trial would demonstrate the most comfortable, practical clothing styles for each season, and society then would produce this clothing year in and year out for its members. Of course, from time to time better fabrics or improved footgear materials might be developed, and some changes might be made in the standard clothing patterns. However, for the most part clothing styles would not change much from one decade to another. In this manner, everyone would be clothed in the most comfortable and healthiest manner at moderate cost. However, this never occurs, for one of the main tools of Peck Order is fashion. By the use of fashion, clothing styles change every year so that the superior groups can demonstrate that they have money enough to buy the new clothing and thus show their superiority to the lower groups. Of course, the secondary groups scramble to imitate the top groups, and the tertiary groups under them imitate the secondary groups, and so on down the Peck Order. Women's dresses and hats, men's suits and headgear, bathing suits, sportswear and all the lesser ornaments to cover nudity are in a state of continual change. No sooner has one new fashion been established than a new one has started at the top of the Peck Order and spreads a wave of economic competition through the entire social structure.

People go through astonishing agony for the sake of fashion. One year women wear dresses with hemlines so high that they cannot sit down in public without danger of indecent exposure, and the next year they hobble themselves in gunnysacks that circle their calves. They cram themselves into tight trousers that defy the law of physics which states that a finite space cannot contain an object larger than itself, and the next year they are wearing ankle-length, loose Turkish harem trousers. Womens' shoes are a form of insanity in a class by themselves. All orthopedists declare that high-heeled shoes defy every principle of healthy footgear. Nevertheless, the ladies push their heels higher or lower, thinner or wider, and develop foot pain, low back pain, swaybacked posture and other chronic disabilities in their frantic scramble to be fashionable and to stay high in the Peck Order.

Men's clothing oscillates similarly, but in a somewhat less blatant manner, for one of the men's favorite illusions is that fashion is a form of folly restricted to women. Double-breasted suits give way to single-breasted suits, and then shift back again. Trousers lose their cuffs one year only to recover them a year or two later, and lapels and trousers narrow and widen with predictable regularity. However, the favorite fashionable appendage of men is the necktie. On the surface, it would seem that not even Peck Order could drive people to devise so inane a piece of apparel as a necktie, a narrow rope of cloth around the neck which chokes and chafes a man and serves no useful, practical purpose whatsoever. It merely circles his neck like a noose and hangs limply down in front of him. However, the necktie is man's most useful agent in fashion. He can flaunt changing patterns, fabrics, styles, widths and lengths. Designs shift from blatant solid colors to pictures of mermaids, from Scottish tartans to Balinese designs, from Indian totems to Manhattan skyscrapers. The successful Peck Order male must have ties carrying the names of the latest fashionable designers, who may be Italian countesses or English peers.

America's favorite Peck Order ritual is the yearly change of automobile models. At staggering cost and enormous expenditures of human labor, which could be used for doing something much more practical, the models of all automobiles change every year. Factories are retooled, advertising campaigns are mounted, and merchandising techniques are revamped, and the cost of cars goes up to support all this. In a rational society, the safest, most comfortable, most efficient type of car would be discovered after a few years, and changes in design then would occur only when significant technical progress occurred. Even then, technical progress rarely would change exterior designs. Cars would be much cheaper, safer and more comfortable. People would keep their cars for four or five years and would buy new ones only when the old ones began to have multiple defects. However, this rational, safe, economical scheme would defy the fundamental principle of society, Peck Order, and hence it would be doomed to failure. People must have new-model cars every year to demonstrate to other people that they can afford to buy them, or at least to make the time payments required to buy them, and thus demonstrate their prominence in the Peck Order. Hence, cars lengthen and then shorten, grow gaudy grillwork and then shed it, look one year like airplanes and the next year like speedboats, sprout huge fenders and then lose them entirely, and alter their shapes in a hundred different ways from year to year. Strange names with exotic sounds are given to these creations. The worst Peck Order players in the automobile field are men. "I keep my Cadillacs for two years before I trade them in," one strategist mentions to another, "because I am conservative with cars." The other counterattacks with "I stick to Lincoln Continentals and trade them in every year; the man at my garage says you save money on repair bills that way." In this way the Peck Order strategist flings his affluence in his friend's face with the innocent air of a man trying to show how thrifty he is.

Vacations are excellent tools for Peck Order strategists. Middle-aged American women stagger through miles of Italian art galleries looking at pictures they do not understand, when they would much rather be visiting friends on a lakeshore a few hundred miles from their homes. Hundreds of thousands of Americans each year wander through those dreary piles of medieval masonry known as European cathedrals when they would be much happier playing golf in Virginia or fishing in Colorado. No region of the globe is safe from American Peck Order vacationers. African tribes are stunned by the sudden appearance of American tourists at their hut doors, Indian villagers gaze in awe at troops of sweating, determined pleasure-seekers, and Balkan peasants are convinced that Americans who career through their countryside in August must be spies, as their governments say; they can think of no other rational reason why anyone would travel there. Little do these benighted natives of the nooks and crannies of the world realize that they are watching one of the most awesome spectacles on the globe, the American Peck Order system in full operation.

Peck Order permeates every aspect of life, from cocktails to colleges. Some Peck Order strategists are continually engaged in developing expensive, ingenious new ways to get drunk. They ransack every hamlet of the globe to find new ingredients for cocktails. Peck Order influences where people send their children to school, as they seek "prestige" colleges and universities. Peck Order even enters into choices of professions. Aspiring suburban families cram their sons into law schools, but plumbers and bricklayers, on a statistical average, make more money, and building people's houses can be more satisfying work than profiting by their legal miseries.

However, Peck Order has its tragic aspects. It causes riots in ghettos as bitter people at the bottom of the Peck Order use chaotic protests to try to get some of the things the people above them have. Peck Order causes people to steal for money, to lie for money, and even at times to kill for money. Half the crime and misery of the world arises directly or indirectly from Peck Order. However, no one really wants to abolish Peck Order; each one merely wants to rise in it.

Different Breed of Cat

Just as individual adolescents may carry out the stratagem Different Breed of Cat, described in Chapter 4, to demonstrate their rejection of their parents by assuming completely different standards and ways of life, large social groups may react to their alienation from the general social body by assuming different customs, different behavior, different moral standards and different goals.

When a large social group carries out a stratagem of Different Breed of Cat, it usually is rebelling against a society which has not accepted it and has forced it into a new role to preserve its sense of dignity and worth. Social Different Breed of Cat may be benign, but often it is malignant, for it splits society into groups that are separated by increasingly wider gulfs, and the social groups that are isolated from each other develop further misunderstandings. Their hostility toward one another occasionally may erupt into civil violence. In our time, the most striking stratagems of Different Breed of Cat have been caused by age differences and racial differences. In former times religious and political forces pushed people into Different Breed of Cat, but in modern America these forces have abated as causes of Cat stratagems.

Adolescents, as a vast social group, are carrying out the most striking stratagem of Different Breed of Cat based on age difference. American family life has become much less cohesive in the last three or four decades. Divorce breaks up twenty-five percent of all marriages, and ten to twenty percent of children are reared in homes in which one of the parents is not the natural father or mother. A large part of the national work force now consists of mothers who work outside the home, leaving the home without a parent in it forty or more hours each week. The automobile and increased affluence have moved people out of the home into bowling alleys, clubs, drive-in movies, drive-in restaurants and dozens of other places as family members restlessly seek the distractions which easy transportation and jingling money make possible.

Moreover, at the beginning of this century the majority of the population lived on farms in cohesive family groups, and many rural families rarely traveled more than twenty-five miles from their homes. In the last three to four decades, with the mechanization of agriculture, the greater part of the rural population has migrated into large metropolitan areas where family unity has been sapped by immersion into a stream of fast-flowing activities, with the majority of the family members spending most of their daylight hours outside the home working or attending school. In addition, each year twenty percent of the American people change their residences as companies transfer personnel over the nation once every two to five years, as families flee the cities for the suburbs, and as shifting economic opportunities draw people from one region of the country to another. As these forces have weakened family unity, the segment which feels most split off and isolated is the adolescent, and they have begun a wild stratagem of Different Breed of Cat which leaves their parents puzzled and anguished.

Different Breed of Cat adolescents adopt different grooming. The boys let their hair creep down their necks and tumble over their shoulders. Both sexes dress in skintight clothing which makes their parents wince, and fads of blatant colors, new styles of exotic clothing and strange ornaments sweep through the adolescent ranks. They dress differently, and they groom themselves differently from the rest of society as they strive to show that they are a Different Breed of Cat, independent of the culture which they feel has rejected them and which they in turn reject in a defiant bid for individuality and self-esteem.

The adolescents also have adopted a new code of sexual mores. They have thrown over the older concepts of sexual restraint and have evolved their own code of sexual freedom. They have devised finely graded but clearly defined stages of intimacy; these stages are, in order of increasing seriousness, (a) dating, (b) going steady, (c) getting serious, (d) getting pinned, (e) getting engaged and (f) getting married. Trial living together may occur somewhere in the latter part of this spectrum of increasing intimacy, and sexual intercourse frequently begins somewhere between going steady and getting engaged. The more extreme adolescents join hippie groups in the large cities. They use marijuana and other intoxicants to get new sensations which take them briefly out of awareness of the culture they are defying. They descend into the streets to champion their own special social and political projects. They develop a slang language of their own. Most basic of all, they feel they are a separate group and that they are removed from the rest of society. The family is dead! Long live the Cats.

The Negroes constitute another social group that has been playing Different Breed of Cat in our society in recent years. Shunned, deprecated, deprived and ignored, they have been blocked off into their own neighborhoods and their own social groups. Their massive migration from Southern farms to Northern slums has given them a new sense of isolation from the whites and a cohesiveness among themselves. Living close to white affluence in large cities has given them a bitter feeling of inferiority and deprivation. Hence, the theme of some segments of the Negro population has become "If we can't be like you, we'll be completely different," and they have sought identity and self-esteem in Different Breed of Cat. For example, the Black Muslims have raised the banners of Islam in the ghettos of New York, Chicago and Los Angeles. Names from the *Arabian Nights* adorn American Negroes in Baltimore and Newark, and a few of them adopt the costumes of the bazaars of Cairo and Damascus. They preach a sacred war of hatred against the infidel white man and vaunt the superiority of *their* religion against the weakness of *his* religion.

Negro adolescents, the most bitter and isolated segment of the

Negro group, dress in their own special manner and develop a slang language all their own. They are isolated both from their own families and from the dominant white society. Unemployed and poorly educated, they are a burden to their families and they find no place in the white man's economic and social system. In return, they scorn the white man's laws, his economic customs and his property. They riot in the white man's streets, loot his stores, battle his police and defy his ideals of social organization. They combine the stratagems of Different Breed of Cat and Temper Tantrum and strew the midnight streets with destruction and death.

Other Negroes grope for new ideologies and new ways of life to get a sense of worth and individuality in other forms of Different Breed of Cat. Politicians, city planners, philanthropists, sociologists, businessmen and the puzzled citizenry wonder how to get rid of Different Breed of Cat. Different Breed of Cat forces Negroes and whites increasingly wider apart and both groups look at each other with less comprehension and more repugnance. The obvious solution, of course, is to treat all Cats alike so that some of them do not have to work so hard at being Different. However, this solution relies heavily on reason and lightly on emotion, and this is always a difficult way to approach the solution of any human problem.

Index